T0302726

on track ...

Nightwish

every album, every song

Simon McMurdo

SONICBOND

sonicbondpublishing.com

Sonicbond Publishing Limited
www.sonicbondpublishing.co.uk
Email: info@sonicbondpublishing.co.uk

First Published in the United Kingdom 2023
First Published in the United States 2023

British Library Cataloguing in Publication Data:
A Catalogue record for this book is available from the British Library

ISBN 978-1-78952-270-9

Typeset in ITC Garamond & ITC Avant Garde
Printed and bound in England

Graphic design and typesetting: Full Moon Media

Follow us on social media:

Twitter: https://twitter.com/SonicbondP

Instagram: https://www.instagram.com/sonicbondpublishing_/

Facebook: https://www.facebook.com/SonicbondPublishing/

Linktree QR code:

on track ...

Nightwish

every album, every song

Simon McMurdo

SONICBOND

sonicbondpublishing.com

Dedications

To Lisa, who helped me realise that there was more to music than Britney and B*Witched. Sorry for stealing your Within Temptation CD when you were at work ...

To David, who heard his neighbour liked Evanescence and gave him a copy of Wishmaster by Nightwish. Look at the monster you've created!

And to Matt, who believed in my enthusiasm back when a podcast was an idea floated at a Horse and Jockey quiz night. He also proofread one of these chapters, so any typos can be blamed on him.

on track ...

Nightwish

Contents

Introduction

Gathered around a campfire in the chilly heart of Kitee, a young Tuomas Holopainen embarked upon a musical venture that would remap his entire life. Nightwish would become one of the biggest musical artists to hail from Finland, and whilst they may have peddled intentions of a casual acoustic-led hobby, the group pretty soon became one of the mightiest forces in the more-is-more sphere of symphonic metal.

From the initial stripped-back brief, the band cycled through formative years as a power metal troupe before leaning into the bombastic allure of cinematic film scores, always remaining loyal to their metal roots. Decades into a tremendous career, recent albums have seen Nightwish edging towards a progressive rock sound and tackling grand lyrical explorations of evolution, astronomy, and the awe of the natural world.

Holopainen's compositions once sought answers to life's big questions, scouring religion and theology in his work as well as mining his own personal experiences and angst. Years later, it seems that the composer is beginning to answer the enquiries of his younger self by tuning in to the natural world and scrutinising the works of revered biologists Charles Darwin and Richard Dawkins. Yet, be it the naïve fantasy of his earlier work or the zealous environmentalism of the later years, an all-encompassing awe has been the through-line of his arrangements, with an almost tangible magic seeping from every output under the Nightwish name.

The stunning voice of Tarja Turunen, a classically trained soprano, set the band apart from their peers from the very start of their career. At a time when women in metal were still a rarity, the unfamiliarity of her vocal style made even more heads turn. Yet, the acclaim came not only for her voice but also the band's unpredictable and masterful compositions, just as happy to turn out inimitable classics such as 'Sleeping Sun' and 'Nemo' alongside expansive epics including the career-defining 'Ghost Love Score' and the mournful drama of 'Dead Boy's Poem'.

Following Tarja's dismissal, Nightwish expanded their audience even further with their second vocalist, Anette Olzon. A strikingly different voice, there was a charming warmth to Anette's delivery that straddled both purity and a cutting strength. Olzon was a perfect addition to the band's more commercial singles and purposely very different from the beloved Turunen. Following her own exit after two records with Nightwish, the band seemed to strike for the best of both worlds with Floor Jansen, a singer just as familiar with soaring operatic pieces as she is with belting and even the occasional death growl.

In a satisfying alignment of growing success and ambition, Nightwish seem to broaden the scope of possibility with every album. A collaboration with the London Philharmonic Orchestra, an entire feature film to support an album, a full instrumental suite ... the band's boundless aspirations never failed to pique the interest of even the most casual of metal enthusiasts.

Yet, whilst their music and reach has expanded, behind the scenes, the band have also tackled the two vocalist firings that threatened to end their career at its peak as well as multiple high-profile exits. The relentlessly personal songwriting from mastermind Tuomas Holopainen skirts none of the issues – from the pressing atmosphere of *Century Child* to the intermittent anger and sorrow of *Dark Passion Play*, Nightwish is not only a vehicle of tremendous ambition but also an unflinching insight into the band's main composer.

It hasn't always been an easy path for Nightwish, but the ride has been immense.

Angels Fall First (1997)

Personnel:
Tero Kinnunen: engineer, mixing
Mika Jussila: mastering
Esa Lehtinen: flutes
Emppu Vuorinen: guitars, bass, acoustic
Tarja Turunen: vocals
Jukka Nevalainen: drums, percussions
Tuomas Holopainen: synths and vocals
Recorded by Tero Kinnunen at Kitee Huvikeskus studio
Recorded between April and May 1997 ('The Carpenter', 'Astral Romance', 'Angels Fall First', 'Nymphomaniac Fantasia', 'Lappi') and September 1997 ('Elvenpath', 'Beauty and the Beast', 'Tutankhamen', 'Know Why The Nightingale Sings')
Produced by Tuomas Holopainen and Nightwish
Arranged by Tuomas Holopainen and Tero Kinnunen
Tero Kinnunen: engineer, mixing
Mika Jussila: mastering
Toni Härkönen: band photography
Garry Black: cover photo

For a band known for their maximalism, it may come as a surprise that Nightwish began as an acoustic venture back in 1996. The man behind it all was Tuomas Holopainen, then playing keyboards in a number of bands, including session work with the black metal outfit Darkwoods My Betrothed. Wearing his inspirations proudly on his sleeve, the Norwegian atmospheric group The 3rd and the Mortal were a clear influence as Tuomas insisted that a female vocalist was a must. With Erno 'Emppu' Vuorinen on guitars and a vocalist Tarja Turunen sourced via their shared music teacher Plamen Dimov, the trio set to work on their first three-track demo. It was then that an opportunity, or indeed a potential spanner in the works, was highlighted: Tarja's unexpected voice. Tuomas commented in the biography *Once Upon a Nightwish*:

> It was such a shock for us when she started singing. I thought we were going to hear a clear, young, beautiful, girly voice … instead, Tarja had a high-pitched, bombastic voice that was already very dramatic and classical … People often think the whole concept was carefully planned. Like – take some heavy metal, add some atmospheric sounds, and throw in some opera vocals – but I can honestly say it was just pure luck

The band's name was shared with a track on the demo and served as a fitting moniker for their atmospheric aspirations. The Nightwish demo is the true taste of that acoustic campfire sound the band aimed for initially. It may seem confusing for many listeners who hear them hark back to their early intentions, though, only to listen to *Angels Fall First* which, whilst certainly not as complex or bombastic as their later material, isn't fully committed to that acoustic world either.

If Tarja's inclusion was a happy accident, Nightwish's metal steer might also have never surfaced had it not been for the band's eventual manager, Ewo Pohjola. Working in A&R for Finnish label Spinefarm, when Tuomas approached him with the band's second demo, Ewo insisted on some heavier inclusions if the group were to be picked up by the metal record label. It was this that Tuomas delivered, and a contract was signed with Spinefarm soon after.

With drummer Jukka Nevalainen already onboard, the band's debut album *Angels Fall First* was released the following year. It turned over just what Spinefarm had requested; from the excitable power metal of the opener 'Elvenpath' to the celebratory 'Know Why the Nightingale Sings', much more fitting for a dance around the campfire than any sedate singalong.

Whilst the album set firm foundations for the band's future career, *Angels Fall First* does suffer when it comes to its identity. The debut was peppered with the band's acoustic origins, such as on the title track and the bookends of the four-part closer 'Lappi', yet the metal guitars and haunting synths were certainly pushed to the fore elsewhere, perhaps a better compliment to Tarja's striking operatic delivery. Lyrically, the songs flit between Tolkien tributes, religious nods, Disney musings and a brief venture to Egypt – a little jumbled perhaps, but the record was anything but predictable.

The final element of 'Lappi' was a reworked version of 'Etiäinen', the only demo track that made the cut into the band's first full length and a fitting pause at the end of the record to reflect back to their humble beginnings. Already the Finns were transforming their sound as opportunities gave rise to their broadening ambitions.

'Elvenpath' 4:38 (Music: Nightwish, lyrics: Tuomas Holopainen)
A campy spoken-word introduction and lyrics unashamedly pulling from Tolkien's *Lord of the Rings* – who would have guessed upon listening to 'Elvenpath' that it was the first step in an astonishing career for one of Finland's biggest musical exports? There is a naivety to the lyrics of the album's opener, warmly enveloped by the power metal genre that was already closely tied to the world of fantasy. Though Tuomas later confessed that this particular set of lyrics never fails to bring a knowing smile to his face, it is a strong opening to *Angels Fall First*. One of the most instant tracks on offer and one of the few that stands up alongside the band's more bombastic later output, the latter evident when it was lifted from the archives over twenty years after its release for the *Decades* tour.

The lyrics lean heavily on *Lord of the Rings*, Tuomas proudly admitting to *MetalElite* that 'Tolkien is my God!', but elsewhere 'Elvenpath' also references Nightwish's home-country with nods to the Finnish forest spirit Tapio and goddess of the hunt, Mielikki. Perhaps the most obvious and innately Finnish reference of the entire track, however, is home gnome's request for Tarja to 'keep the sauna warm for him'.

Endearing as the song may be, it also should be recognised how many of the themes explored here would go on to become staples in Nightwish's future releases. The magic of imagination explored in-depth on *Imaginaerum*, the reverence of nature that *Human. :||: Nature.* drew upon and a further venture into fantasy on *Wishmaster*. Perhaps, despite its unassuming youthful innocence, 'Elvenpath' was a fitting first chapter in the Nightwish story after all.

'Beauty and the Beast' 6:22 (Music: Nightwish, lyrics: Tuomas Holopainen)

Tuomas Holopainen may well be the lifeforce of Nightwish, the constant beating heart behind the band's ethos and songwriting, but a vocalist he is not – by his own admission too, we should recognise. Still, needs must in the early days of the band, and he stepped up to the microphone for the duet 'Beauty and the Beast'. It isn't that Tuomas sounds terrible, but his relatively nasal delivery lacks dynamism, and his shortcomings are thoroughly amplified when going toe-to-toe with Tarja, a vocalist already demonstrating her immense vocal prowess.

One of the most impactful tracks on the debut, 'Beauty and the Beast' stood proud on the live circuit and was given the prized spot of closing out the setlist during the band's first Finnish tour. Standing the test of time, it also made a reappearance during the *Century Child* tour, with fans regularly pining for a further live resurrection, if only to hear future vocalist Floor Jansen's take.

The title may refer most directly to the famous Disney film, but it was also coined in the gothic metal scene to describe an angelic female voice juxtaposed with grunts, growls, or screams. Very apt for Nightwish, who, at the beginning of their career, were often categorised amongst peers such as Norway's Theatre of Tragedy, the dictionary definition of the beauty and the beast style. Tuomas likely wasn't too put-out by the comparison, though, reflecting in early interviews with *BraveWords*: 'Theatre of Tragedy was a big influence to me at the time when I was starting with Nightwish, together with other female-fronted metal acts like The 3rd and the Mortal and The Gathering'.

'The Carpenter' 5:56 (Music: Nightwish, lyrics: Tuomas Holopainen)

As the first single from Nightwish, 'The Carpenter' was part of a split release with fellow Finnish metallers Children of Bodom and the black metal project Thy Serpent. The midtempo will no doubt have stood out against these heavier inclusions, particularly Tarja's pure vocal – a striking counterpart to the death growls elsewhere on the release.

The title refers to arguably the most well-known carpenter in history, Jesus Christ. Rather than an evangelical hymn or a blasphemous attack, the perspective of the lyrics observes the story of sacrifice from the sidelines. Subsequent interviews, however saw Tuomas a little more critical of religious ideology as he described the track to *Eternity* magazine as: 'a very dismal and bitter song as far as the lyrics are concerned. It deals with my aspects over religious issues and the hypocrisy, which is a spreading disease in today's world'.

The music video distances itself from any obvious Christian symbolism, steering towards Greek mythology, and the story of Icarus as a man is shown constructing his own wings before leaping to an uncertain fate before the sunset. The video is interspersed with a typically '90s shot of Tarja standing in front of a blurry PlayStation 1-style backdrop, planting it firmly as a product of its time.

'The Carpenter' began a love affair between Tuomas and religious iconography that would persist for albums to come but is perhaps, alongside *Oceanborn*'s 'Gethsemane', the most obvious take on biblical scriptures. Decades later, Tuomas commented to *MetalBlast*:

> When I wrote 'The Carpenter' I was still praying, and I'm not praying anymore. That's why there are songs like 'Tribal' (on *Human. :||: Nature.)* and 'Weak Fantasy' (on *Endless Forms Most Beautiful*). It's an evolution in personality and an evolution in music.

Hindsight sees the track pale when compared to the refined compositions that would come after it, especially in regard to the band's finely curated lead singles, so perhaps it's a surprise that 'The Carpenter' still managed a respectable level of success in Finland, peaking at number three in the charts and re-entering the top ten following the more considerable success of *Oceanborn*.

The final redemption for the song came with its inclusion on the *Decades* tour, an unexpected treat for long-time fans but a fond farewell to the track, too, as Holopainen confirmed it would be the song's last live outing. Thankfully for many, Tuomas had long since hung up his microphone and his vocal parts were reinterpreted by future band member Troy Donockley. Admittedly, the two share a similar vocal tone, though it must be conceded that Donockley gave a superior performance than Holopainen had managed back in 1997.

'Astral Romance' 5:11 (Music: Nightwish, lyrics: Tuomas Holopainen)
For a third track in a row, Holopainen takes on vocal duties. Akin to 'Beauty and the Beast', 'Astral Romance' operates as a conversation between two lovers, though this macabre story is much more in line with *Romeo and Juliet* than Belle and the Prince as the two are ultimately separated by

death. Although, one interpretation could be that the death in the song is actually their reunion, reframing the longing finale lyric 'I shall desire you forevermore' as a romantic promise rather than a mournful aching.

Doomy guitar riffs make the song a striking highlight from the album, a sound that also helps 'Astral Romance' to stand out amongst the band's entire discography to date. Whilst Tuomas has asserted that doom metal is an influence on Nightwish, it's only occasionally been evidenced in their actual output – namely on 2020's 'Endlessness' and briefly during *Imaginaerum*'s 'Rest Calm'. Here, there is no better companion to the woe of the bittersweet song than the macabre leaning of the genre that birthed metal giants such as My Dying Bride and Katatonia. Jukka Nevalainen agreed, picking it out as an early personal favourite when he became involved with the group in the late '90s.

Whilst Tarja and Tuomas played their unmatched romance on the *Angels Fall First* version, Holopainen would couple Turunen off with Sonata Arctica's Tony Kakko for a later remake on *Over the Hills and Far Away*. If any song from *Angels Fall First* deserved a second shot following the band's growing success, it's hard to begrudge it being this one.

'Angels Fall First' 5:34 (Music: Nightwish, lyrics: Tuomas Holopainen)
No other song on the debut album ties itself as closely to the band's demo than 'Angels Fall First'. Excluding the final third, it's a stripped-back acoustic affair and is surely the prime example of their original intended brief. The stirring track is a capture of grief and a testament to Tarja's exceptional talent for emotion as she pines through every word. Fittingly, the song swells into something entirely different for its closing third as the grief gives way to conviction and a path through the suffering is illuminated.

Later Nightwish records would need to dedicate pages of the album liner notes to acknowledge its contributors, but *Angels Fall First* need offer only a single musical acknowledgement outside of the band themselves. Esa Lehtinen was a friend of Holopainen and played brass in the same military band. On 'Angels Fall First', he switched to woodwind and his flute can be heard across numerous tracks, though few centre it as beautifully as on this title track. The delicate flute solo precedes a denser, synth-heavy closing section, underlining the persistent ache of the question asked: 'Oh, Lord… why the angels fall first?'

'Tutankhamen' 5:30 (Music: Nightwish, lyrics: Tuomas Holopainen)
Whilst later albums placed a clear focus on cohesion, flitting from elves to Jesus to Egyptian pharaohs gave the band's debut a more disjointed feel. The less than imaginative 'Tutankhamen' also feels like a distant memory for the conscious songwriter that Holopainen would become, making references to pyramids, Howard Carter, and the valley of the kings. A minor curveball is chanted in the chorus as Tarja wills Tutankhamen to accompany her through

a stargate wormhole, convincing many that the song was at least slightly inspired by the TV franchise *Stargate*. Lending credence to the rumours, *Stargate* SG-*1* first aired in July 1997, whilst 'Tutankhamen' was amongst four of the album's tracks that were not committed to tape until September of the same year. It seems Tutankhamen's secrets continue to unfold ...

If nothing else, the track serves as a welcome burst of energy, particularly following the ballads and midtempos before it. It's also somewhat refreshing in its simplicity: no complex metaphors, just a simple song of love and longing for a long-dead pharaoh. Surely we can all relate to that?

'Nymphomaniac Fantasia' 4:45 (Music: Nightwish, lyrics: Tuomas Holopainen)

Nightwish lyrics evoke a variety of reactions amongst loyal fans: awe, euphoria, even a healthy dose of misery. Yet, 'Nymphomaniac Fantasia' may be the sole track in the band's discography that generates as many stifled giggles as it does banging heads. 'The scent of a woman was not mine' Tarja sings as the track sets the scene of a scorned lover. With the dramatic synths in the mid-section, 'Nymphomaniac Fantasia' is musically one of the grandest statements on *Angels Fall First*, albeit often dismissed for its peculiar storyline and that unforgettable closing line: 'Deeper shall be the wound between your legs'. Eek.

It's these lines that Tuomas confessed, only a year later, were far from his best work, commenting to *Entry* magazine:

> I have few excuses. I've always felt that infidelity and disloyalty are one the worst sins mankind has created, and these things make me angry and sad. So I wanted to express those feelings again in a musical form, but the result turned out rather funny. Lyrics and music don't work the way they should, but the language at the end of the song is always good for a laugh – even if I didn't mean it.

'Know Why the Nightingale Sings' 4:13 (Music: Nightwish, lyrics: Tuomas Holopainen)

Finally, a chance for guitarist Emppu Vuorinen to let loose! The star of this particular show snatches the spotlight with a liberating solo, emerging as Tarja sings her final note. It's the most obvious predecessor of the power metal influence that swept the albums to follow and a final romp before the more experimental 'Lappi'.

The song establishes an enquiring perspective that would persist throughout Tuomas' earlier compositions until on *Endless Forms Most Beautiful* and *Human. :||: Nature.*, a more experienced Holopainen would begin to answer the questions put forth by his younger self following deep dives into the work of Whitman and Darwin. It is a satisfying full-circle moment that loops the curious, explorative youngsters of 1996 with their wiser, accomplished future selves.

The title of the song was lifted from a conversation Tuomas had with his sister Susanna when asking why she enjoyed parachute jumping. Her response, 'why does the nightingale sing?', became the title and a lyrical theme that can be read as a direct tribute to his sister's hobby ('dancing with the spirit of the air') or an expression of freedom and heeding our own urges ('taking a step to a world unbound').

'Lappi (Lapland)': I. 'Erämaajärvi' 2:15, II. 'Witchdrums' 1:19, III. 'This Moment Is Eternity' 3:12, IV. 'Etiäinen' 2:34 (Music: Nightwish, lyrics: Tuomas Holopainen)

Lappi, in many ways, should be considered Tuomas' first epic. Tracks such as 'Ghost Love Score', 'The Greatest Show on Earth' and 'The Poet and the Pendulum' would go on to become Nightwish staples and compositional peaks for Holopainen, yet here is where it all began with a nine-minute, multi-part saga.

Kindly translating the title for non-Finnish speakers, 'Lappi' takes inspiration from Lapland, the northernmost area of Finland, and seizes the purity of the chilling and striking landscapes. 'Lappi' opens with 'Erämaajärvi', roughly translated to 'Wilderness Lake', and the journey begins with a sparse arrangement, luring us into the tense 'Witchdrums', unnerving and gripping despite its short runtime. The beating heart of 'Lappi' arrives, unsurprisingly, when it allows itself more time to resonate – 'This Moment is Eternity' is the only element to incorporate the band's metal sound, wielding it perfectly to a deliver a riveting peak. Finally, the one track lifted from the demo 'Etiäinen' closes out with an atmospheric mix of vocalisations and acoustic strumming.

It was a strange decision to split up the tracks of Lappi into individual songs, though it's likely that Spinefarm were simply not used to an entire song suite being tossed into their laps. Perhaps the marketing bods were also keen to give the impression of a lengthier record to appeal to more buyers. Either way, from a listener's standpoint, segregating the tracks gives the false impression that elements such as 'Witchdrums' and 'Erämaajärvi' could standalone outside the wider piece. In reality, both serve to lose a lot of their charm and purpose when taken outside of the scope of 'Lappi' as anyone experiencing them on a Spotify shuffled playlist can attest to. Future songs such as *Century Child*'s 'Beauty of the Beast' would rectify this and, whilst outlining the separate song sections in the booklet and tracklisting, would unite them into one track on the release, ensuring all the pieces of the puzzle remain connected.

The intent was clear from Holopainen's ambition on 'Lappi'. Even when backed only by a small band and a flautist, the sonic variation of the closing track and the ability to knit together hugely different segments gave a quiet drive to Tuomas that would help shape the masterful epics that lay in the composer's future. 24 years into that very future, the band would return to snowy climes on the second disc of *Human. :||: Nature.* on 'Lappi's distant aural cousin 'Quiet as the Snow'. Whilst it would inevitably have been transformed beyond recognition, it does beg the question – how monumental could 'Lappi' have been with resources made available to them years later? And yet, at the same time, what a tragedy it would have been to have never heard this formidable first stab from a young composer swelling in both confidence and skill.

'Nightwish (Demo)' 5:49 (Music: Nightwish, lyrics: Tuomas Holopainen)

'Nightwish' would have to wait a decade for a commercial release, eventually emerging as part of the 2007 Spinefarm reloaded re-releases and later as the final track of the 2018 *Decades* compilation. Still, it holds quite the honour as the song that gave the band their name back in the mid-'90s and was a fundamental part of the latter compilation, rounding out their reverse-retrospective with the humble beginnings that had swelled into the ambitious group of two decades later.

The droning synth that was repurposed as the intro to 'Elvenpath' and the sharp synth bursts that characterised 'Beauty and the Beast' suggest that 'Nightwish' emerged as the band's sound evolved, transitioning from an acoustic focus to something more layered and complex. Although sounding understandably less refined than on later albums, the strength of Tarja's voice was already evident in their elevation of the sparse guitar-vocal verses – on the spoken word outro, however, she is almost unrecognisable. In the short period between the demo and album, an astounding growth was already apparent when that same meek voice would transform into the commanding narrator inviting us to take a stroll down the 'Elvenpath'.

'The Forever Moments (Demo)' 5:36 (Music: Nightwish, lyrics: Tuomas Holopainen)

'The Forever Moments' is the true lost gem of the band's demo – despite the Spinefarm revisited release, it never received the *Decades* boost of 'Nightwish', nor the *Angels Fall First* makeover of 'Etiäinen'. A shame, too, as it is possibly the most accessible of the three; a timeless piano melody ushering through the verses to a powerful hook of Tarja's vocalisations.

The lyrics of 'The Forever Moments' deal with the passage of time, trapped in the sad nostalgic realisation that things will never be the same. Time can be taken as the villain of the story – turning swans back to ugly ducklings, howls to distant echoes – but with a persistent focusing on the losses, the final lyrics suddenly find us lulled to eternal sleep. It could be a gloomy telling of our misplaced focus, or perhaps a precursor to the band's later message of mindful presence and embracing the here and now.

Though not widely accessible, at least not before the dawn of the internet, the song was offered as a treat to loyalists in 2002 when the three demo tracks, 'Nightwish', 'Etiäinen' and 'The Forever Moments', were presented for download during the *Century Child* era. Already a complete metamorphosis having taken place in the band, the three songs sounded worlds away from *Century Child*'s fledgling bombast, giving a fascinating insight into the early days for the growing Nightwish audience.

'Once Upon a Troubadour' 5:20 (Music: Nightwish, lyrics: Tuomas Holopainen)

It's been a bumpy road for 'Once Upon a Troubadour'. Amongst the songs that Tuomas presented to Spinefarm's Ewo, the collection of early tracks was labelled a decent first stab but needing more work. The track's time would come with the initial release of *Angels Fall First* when it graced the main tracklist on the first run of a limited 500 copies. When *Angels Fall First* was distributed more widely, however, the track was cut in favour of four additional songs – 'Beauty and the Beast', 'Tutankhamen', 'Know Why the Nightingale Sings' and 'Elvenpath'.

The song itself is a simple romance story of a travelling bard falling in love with a servant girl whom he takes as a partner. The song fittingly strips back to a harpsichord solo and returns to the acoustic-oriented sound explored elsewhere; even Tuomas' vocals don't sound too jarring, though a cheerful, charismatic bard he is not.

'Once Upon a Troubadour's most telling message comes in the final line when the chorus alternates to: 'sing with us the tales which the music will keep alive', observing the immortality of music as it is passed down over time. As Holopainen revisited bardic tradition, it wouldn't have been immodest for him to wonder if his own songs and legacy would go on to outlive him. In 2018, he and his wife Johanna Kurkela (as well as Nightwish's own Troy Donockley) would live the story of the song as they sank further into Celtic and folk music for their project Auri. Far from a servant girl, however, Kurkela also performs as a successful solo artist in Finland. Meanwhile, 'Once Upon a Troubadour's eventual wider release would not come until the French *Wishmastour 2000* compilation and the *Bless the Child* EP, both of which gathered together most of the band's earlier B-sides and bonus tracks. Lucky Korean listeners were able to enjoy the song a little sooner, thanks to its addition to the 1999 Korean release of *Angels Fall First*.

'A Return to the Sea' 5:45 (Music: Nightwish, lyrics: Tuomas Holopainen)

Just like 'Once Upon a Troubadour', 'A Return to the Sea' was originally included in the limited run of *Angels Fall First* before being relegated to bonus track status for future releases. The track tells of trilobites (extinct arthropods), swimming spiders (octopi?) and socially inclined snakes, all observed through the lens of an evolving world. As always, though, the might of mother nature remains successful as the song draws to its fateful conclusion: 'seadrops foam all empty human skulls… the tyrant's return to the sea'.

The song is an early precursor to the 2015 album *Endless Forms Most Beautiful,* when Darwin's theory of evolution was once again mined for inspiration by Holopainen, forming a central theme to the band's later work.

Oceanborn (1998)

Personnel:
Emppu Vuorinen: guitars
Sami Vänskä: bass
Tarja Turunen: vocals
Jukka Nevalainen: drums, percussions
Tuomas Holopainen: synthesizers and piano
Tapio Wilska: vocals ('Devil & The Deep Dark Ocean', 'The Pharaoh Sails To Orion'), backing vocals ('Moondance')
Esa Lehtinen: flute
Plamen Dimov: violin
Kaisli Kaivola: violin
Markku Palola: viola
Erkki Hirvikangas: cello
Recorded by Tero Kinnunen at Caverock studio
Recorded between August to October 1998
Arranged by Nightwish and Tero Kinnunen (except 'Walking in the Air' by Howard Blake)
Mika Jussila: mastering
Mikko Karmila: mixing
Toni Härkönen: band photography
Maria Sandell: cover art (Spinefarm version), inlay art
Markus Mayer: cover art (Drakkar version)

As the years passed, Tuomas reflected on *Angels Fall First* as 'basically an extended demo' which set the scene for a proper Nightwish debut, a second chance at a first impression. That's not to dismiss the success of the first record, however, which still afforded them a headline tour in Finland and has since gone on to sell over 36,000 copies in their home country alone. The success was surely a boost for the unassuming Holopainen, too, now with a well-received debut and record label backing to boot, it's easy to see why *Oceanborn* became so much more ambitious, challenging and considered.

In what has become a Nightwish tradition, Holopainen remained secretive with his early demos. By the time he unveiled his work, only a handful of extracts had been shared with producer Tero Kinnunen. Eventually, Tuomas' knowledge of his bandmates' capabilities improved, evolving into a smoother transition into the studio, in 1998, however, the sessions were described as 'a living hell'. Tarja, in particular, recalls collapsing in tears as the rest of the band failed to comprehend her vocal limitations, challenging the young vocalist with the near-impossible vocal lines written – 'Stargazers' becoming a particular offender.

Whilst the demands may have occasionally been a little much, the scale of what would become *Oceanborn* was a major step-up from its predecessor.

The songs felt tighter, more cohesive and the symphonic elements that would soon become a staple for the band began to surface, thanks in part to the contributions of Plamen Dimov, the teacher that had united the bandmembers years before. Inevitably feeling a wave of pride as he observed his student's musical vision, Dimov was more than happy to let Tuomas steer the ship during the recording sessions. The location for the young composer's metamorphosis? A local sports hall.

The band expanded to include bassist Sami Vänskä who would stick around for the band's power metal days, before being asked to leave Nightwish after the *Wishmaster* era wrapped. Vänskä was lured in by the band's affinity for fellow Finns Stratovarius, a band that Tuomas admitted being a very evident inspiration on an album that was much faster and guitar-driven than *Angels Fall First* had been.

The first taste of this new, refined sound came in the shape of *Oceanborn*'s first single 'Sacrament of Wilderness'. Things couldn't have got off to a better start as the single hit the top of the Finnish charts and was soon certified gold for surpassing sales of 5000. It was an achievement matched by the album's second single, a cover of Howard Blake's festive ballad 'Walking in the Air' from the TV film *The Snowman*. It was viewed by some as a peculiar inclusion for a metal band, but reflecting back, it perfectly suited Tuomas' through-line of imagination and innocence.

Oceanborn dropped in December 1998, slotted between the two single releases. It reached a peak of number 5 in the Finnish charts and also made a dent in the German top 100, helped by the band signing a distribution deal with the German label Drakkar. Over the years, the Nightwish output from the Drakkar label has been, at best, questionable. Handling distribution rights until 2004, their releases include the band's first compilation *Tales from the Elvenpath* – a victim of clunky sequencing, it was at least a handy way to pick up many of the band's B-sides at the time.

Despite their legitimate dealings, though without much input from Tuomas and the band, the Drakkar releases often feel unofficial, though usually with decent cover art at least. Tuomas didn't agree, slating the *Tales from the Elvenpath* cover in the band's biography and questioning Drakkar's decision to commission a redesigned *Oceanborn* cover to Metal Observer:

> We had been very satisfied with the original cover of *Oceanborn*, but the German record company wasn't and decided to have it repainted. I do not like that one at all, it's stupid, it's more like Swampborn or Corpse in The Swamp

If Nightwish fans can thank Drakkar for anything, however, it was their insistence on a new song to mark the 1998 eclipse. The track would become one of the band's first true classics, 'Sleeping Sun', an enduring song that still makes a convincing demand for a setlist spot to this day.

If signing with a record label wasn't evidence enough, the success of *Oceanborn* transformed Nightwish once and for all from a hobby to a viable career, as Tuomas discussed with *Dark Page of Wonders*:

> I had to quit my studies and now I'm a full-time musician and that's just fine with me. It was a very good excuse to quit studies, I had no time for anything else anymore. As a musician, I hope to keep evolving all the time, especially as a songwriter. That's what I hope most for myself. I don't think that I'm so much of a musician or a performer, I'm rather a song-maker, that's the thing that I love and that I want to be.

Nightwish were rapidly expanding their audience as not only Germany, but Europe as a whole began to take notice. The continent may be sizable, but the metal world is well-linked and *Oceanborn* was already making waves for the up-and-comers.

'Stargazers' 4:27 (Music and lyrics: Tuomas Holopainen)
There is a through line from 'A Return to the Sea', the final track on multiple editions of *Angels Fall First*, and our first venture on *Oceanborn* as 'Stargazers' is similarly unbound by time or location. The song complements the album's cover artwork, recasting the earth as an all-seeing eye as 'Stargazers' cites just some of the magnificent sights it has witnessed.

The 'grand oasis' of our world is the 'theatre for the play of life', but this track is also keen to underline just how insignificant humanity is when taken in the context of the vastness of the universe: 'Ephemeral life touched by a billion-year-show'. Once again, Tuomas' fascination with evolution is given an early airing before permeating *Endless Forms Most Beautiful* years later. Naturally, considering the song's title, astronomy is given plenty of airtime, too, including a reference to Ptolemy's second-century treatise 'Almagest', which documents the paths of stars and planets.

A grand theme required an equally resplendent delivery, and much of that was left to Tarja, who demonstrates her finest vocal work to date. The soprano may have sounded leaps and bounds ahead of her work on the band's debut, but it came at a price; 'Stargazers' was just one of the songs that rendered the sessions a living hell for the young vocalist, namely the challenging chorus which was almost impossible to sing.

Unsurprisingly, the song was not a setlist mainstay and was struck from the list of possibilities during Anette Olzon's time with the band. With Floor Jansen onboard, however, the song astonished fans with its return on the *Endless Forms Most Beautiful* world tour, an apt inclusion considering the shared theme. Aware of the appetite for the song, a recording of it was used to promote the *Vehicle of Spirit* live release, but it was the performance in Himos Park that sticks with fans as bassist Sami Vänskä returned to perform the song with Nightwish fifteen years after his departure.

'Gethsemane' 5:21 (Music and lyrics: Tuomas Holopainen)

Holopainen commented in the *Oceanborn* collector's edition booklet that it was during this period he resolved that his life's goal was a career in music. It gives weight to 'Gethsemane's realisation 'I weep to have what I fear to lose'. It would prove to be a plaintive reality for Holopainen as firings and tensions would later threaten to sever him from the band, fast becoming an integral part of his life. Back in 1998, however, a young Tuomas and co were still embarking on making Nightwish something worth losing in the first place.

The album segues effortlessly into its second track, which switches up 'Stargazers' dramatic synths for twinkling keys. The heaviness remains, but the pace drops to midtempo, a respite from the frantic opener and a chance for the reflective set of lyrics to take centre stage. Tuomas has remarked that 'Gethsemane', despite its many religious allusions, is a deeply personal track and particularly singles out the final lyric for its poignancy: 'without you the poetry within me is dead'.

In its purest reading, 'Gethsemane' is an unrequited love song swathed in pious metaphor. The garden of Gethsemane, from which the song takes its title is referenced in the gospels of Matthew and Mark as the location of Jesus' suffering and agony before being betrayed by Judas Iscariot. Indeed, the first verse lifts so many repurposed quotes from the bible itself that God-fearing listeners could easily reinterpret it as a reverent retelling of the biblical story, though an unsung final line in the booklet instead underlines the songwriter's personal longing: 'Let me tell you, a scene can be much more to remember than the play itself'.

'Devil and the Deep Dark Ocean' 4:46 (Music and lyrics: Tuomas Holopainen)

Nothing confirms a metal band's growing success than a '90s satanic panic conspiracy. The group's first real taste of controversy came thanks to this *Oceanborn* cut that, as its title suggests, told a sinister story about evil lurking beneath the waters. All of this was punctuated by ex-Finntroll lead Tapio Wilska and his menacing guest vocals, a world away from Tuomas' own innocuous contributions on *Angels Fall First*.

Tuomas recounts the short-lived drama in *Once Upon a Nightwish*:

> There was a teacher at the Kitee junior high and high school who thought our lyrics were provocative and satanic… she'd translated the lyrics of 'Devil and the Deep Dark Ocean' to Finnish. I saw the letter she had sent to the minister of the Kitee parish and apparently, the Christian circles in Kitee through that we were some kind of Satan worshippers for a while… It was all because of this one song and the fact that there's actually an upside-down cross on the [*Oceanborn*] cover. We hadn't thought about it before that, but then we looked at it and were like, 'Damn, it really is a cross'.

'Devil and the Deep Dark Ocean' was the heaviest cut thus far from Nightwish, only to be surpassed later by another Wilska duet 'The Pharaoh Sails to Orion'. The track revelled in its ominous atmosphere and lost none of its chilling evil when reintroduced on the band's *Decades* tour in 2018. With Floor Jansen and Marco Hietala taking on vocal duties, a live clip was used as a trailer of sorts for the *Decades: Live in Buenos Aires* tour DVD, showing off Jansen's chilling scream at the three-minute mark and the beefed-up orchestrals of Nightwish twenty years on.

'Sacrament of Wilderness' 4:12 (Music and lyrics: Tuomas Holopainen and Emppu Vuorinen)

Oceanborn couldn't have had a better launchpad than the single 'Sacrament of Wilderness' which held the top spot in the Finnish charts for four weeks, eventually being certified gold. It was an unconventional single choice, flagged as such by *Oceanborn*'s mixer Mikko Karmila who pointed out that the chorus doesn't hit for two full minutes. Whilst Karmila praised other tracks, a suitable, accessible entry point into the record was not forthcoming. Fortunately, the group may reflect following the astounding success of the single, it was the one they eventually went with in the end.

Though the band have expressed an intense disappointment with the music video, it remains more uneventful than outright bad. Intended as a standard live performance, budgets were tight – something that is never more apparent than on their YouTube channel, where it pales next to the cinematic clips the band would go on to shoot in the future. Thankfully for Tarja, the top comments on the video seem more enamoured with her voice than her questionable, tight-curled hairstyle of the time.

'Sacrament of Wilderness' is one of the few compositions which feature writing credits from another band member, as Emppu contributed the riff and chorus. Although the group is certainly spearheaded by Holopainen, he has been keen over the years to state that Nightwish remains a democracy and all ideas from all members are considered.

This wasn't quite the case during the *Oceanborn* days, though as Holopainen and Vuorinen had a heated confrontation about Tuomas' higher income, bolstered by his role as composer. Tuomas recalled in *Once Upon a Nightwish*:

> In the early years, I might not have made it clear enough to the others that the songs would be coming from me alone, and that's why these situations occurred. Emppu might've felt bad about his ideas not being used, but then again, he didn't offer anything else but the riff and chorus for 'Sacrament of Wilderness' – and they can be heard on the album.

Improved communication appeased the teething pains of the fledgling band, with Emppu sticking by Tuomas' side as the longest-serving band member throughout Nightwish's career. A welcome wad of royalties from a gold-selling single might have also helped plaster over any tensions too.

Despite its choice as single prompting doubts in Mikko Karmila, 'Sacrament of Wilderness's anthemic chorus is the perfect introduction to the clearer power metal steer of *Oceanborn,* whilst Tarja's vocal lines transform the refrain into an infectious earworm. Putting aside the positives for a second, Marco Hietala would later name the song as one of his least favourites in the band's discography as he commented in the group's *Nightmail* website feature:

> I don't really have anything against it. I can say that there's certain mathematic predictability in the vocal melodies and I find other songs more exciting because they don't have it. It's still a good addition to the live set.

To the live set, it would return for one last time as the *Decades* tour spanned the globe in 2018. It was a fond farewell with Tuomas confirming to *Metal Chest of Wonders* that, just like 'The Carpenter', 'Sacrament of Wilderness' will never be played again following the anniversary outing.

'Passion and the Opera' 4:58 (Music and lyrics: Tuomas Holopainen)
If Tarja's vocal prowess was a surprise in the band's early days, it was recognised as a key selling point on *Oceanborn,* and whilst Tarja described the horrendous recordings as a result of challenging vocal lines, it's hard to believe that anyone else served as a muse for the triumphant 'Passion and the Opera'.

That's not to feed into the persistent unfounded rumours that Tuomas was harbouring a romantic longing for Tarja during their time working together, but it's clear to see how the vocalist and face of the group could fit the role of a lusted-for Goddess as described in the lyrics. And when it comes to songs with an erotic overtone, this track indisputably tramples all over 'Nymphomaniac Fantasia'.

It's in the soaring vocalisations of the song's last two minutes when Tarja sounds particularly striking – both enchanting and haunting in equal measure. The inspiration came from the film *The Fifth Element,* as Tuomas shared with *Morbid Noizz*:

> When I saw this film for the first time, I was enchanted and I remember perfectly well that the same evening I just sat down and composed 'Passion and the Opera'. Film music has always been a great source of inspiration for me and *The Fifth Element* is one of my favourite films. Bombastic elements [and] the majesty of the atmosphere in our compositions comes directly from the world of films and film music.

Tarja herself had a clear fondness for the song as it remained in her solo live set long after her firing from Nightwish – it was a worthy demonstration of just how much her voice had developed since those early years. At the time, 'Passion and the Opera's potential was recognised, and it was selected as a promotional release, backed safely with the enduring single 'Sacrament of Wilderness'.

'Swanheart' 4:44 (Music and lyrics: Tuomas Holopainen)

Thus far, the album had proven to be much more power metal-focused than their debut, but 'Swanheart' was a pared-back interval that ensured the group still stood out from their peers. Tarja was once again front and centre, transforming into a choir of layered vocals in the main refrain. The definition of a power ballad, the drums hit for the second verse and a wailing guitar signals the middle eight, yet it's the striking opening of flutes and piano that give the track its undeniable charm.

When the band embarked on their *Decades* tour, few could have guessed that it would be 'Swanheart' that opened up proceedings. As Troy Donockley emerged onto the stage, pipes in hand, a shortened, instrumental version was the audience's first taste of the setlist celebrating over twenty years of Nightwish.

'Moondance' 3:31 (Music: Tuomas Holopainen)

'Moondance' is *Oceanborn*'s only instrumental and though it works as an uplifting bit, picking up the pace after 'Swanheart', guitarist Emppu was not keen on it being included in the final album. Like dragging an unimpressed relative onto the dancefloor, he was overruled by his band members who vouched for the feel-good jaunt, a timely break from the seriousness that Nightwish had often peddled. The playful keys, emerging from an atmospheric intro, carry us through the piece and before a final crescendo, the track gives way to a flute solo from Esa Lehtinen following his star turn on *Angels Fall First*'s title track and another winning contribution on 'Swanheart'.

Though worlds away from the Celtic folk of the band's later years, the track managed much of the same atmosphere, with gang cheers transporting listeners directly to a cosy pub well after last orders. If any song in the Nightwish catalogue has ever begged for a resurgence with pipe-player Troy Donockley onboard, it's 'Moondance'.

'The Riddler' 5:16 (Music and lyrics: Tuomas Holopainen)

Tuomas would later become fascinated with the loss of innocence, a dominant theme on 2002's *Century Child* in particular. During 'The Riddler', we discover the root of this search as the song casts our purity into the hands of a tricky puzzle maker who warns the listener that ignorance truly is bliss. As the verses cycle through question after question, the response remains that knowledge isn't always as fulfilling as we hope it will be. After all, there remains a satisfaction in not knowing the answer to all of life's mysteries. The ending remains uncertain.

Perhaps the warning is not heeded, as the middle eight resolves 'for nature hates virginity, I wish to be touched', sending the songwriter down a ceaseless path to reclaim what was lost. Or could the later clarity that it's the 'ocean's minds' that are craved be an acceptance that a lifelong journey of learning is the goal? How apt that it's the 'The Riddler' that leaves us guessing.

'The Pharaoh Sails to Orion' 6:27 (Music and lyrics: Tuomas Holopainen)

Before the respite of a familiar cover version, *Oceanborn* unleashes its most perplexing creation – challenging the listener with some of the most inaccessible lyrics in the band's career, at least for those who aren't well versed in Egyptology.

'The Pharaoh Sails to Orion' begins with a spoken bible extract lifted from the book of Exodus in which the Pharaoh threatens Moses to death should he see his face again. From there, it's the Pharaoh that suffers from the plagues put upon him by Moses, followed by his descent (or indeed, ascent) into the afterlife.

Pulling on this religious inception, mixing in the middle English language, and taking place somewhere between the constellations and the Greek mythological underworld, the song challenges 'Elvenpath' for the most expansive points of reference. Yet, whether the story of the song is clear or not doesn't impact the captivating intensity of *Oceanborn*'s heaviest moment, aided once again by the vocal contributions of Tapio Wilska. The song persevered into setlists throughout the *Wishmaster* era, being immortalised on the band's first live release, *From Wishes to Eternity*.

Since *Oceanborn* is the only studio album from Nightwish not to offer some sort of epic composition, 'The Pharaoh Sails to Orion' with its length and unpredictable structure, is as close as it gets. Still, it would be unfair to line it up against the heavy hitters that would follow, such as *Wishmaster*'s 'Dead Boy's Poem' and 'FantasMic', though it did prove to be a winning juxtaposition to the sweeping and equally mercurial 'Lappi'.

'Walking in the Air' 5:28 (Music and lyrics: Howard Blake)

The enduring festive favourite 'Walking in the Air' was an unlikely choice for a power metal band, but Nightwish were always determined to stand out from the pack. Naturally, the song has a heavier climax, but the frosty magic of the Howard Blake original is preserved. One of the best-known versions of 'Walking in the Air' features the voice of the Welsh chorister Aled Jones, who would years later perform the song as a duet alongside Tarja for Finnish TV channel YLE.

Helped by the lengthy Finnish winters, the song not only hit the top spot in the Finnish charts, it also stuck around for eighteen weeks, cementing the band's success in their home country. Tuomas was inevitably elated by the reception as he quoted the 'beautiful and soulful' song as the one piece of music he wished he could have written. His wish may not have come true, but with the song remaining a setlist staple for tours to come including through the Anette years, 'Walking in the Air' soon became an integrated part of their own history as well as its inception as a soundtrack to the beloved Raymond Briggs story *The Snowman*.

'Sleeping Sun' 4:01 (Music and lyrics: Tuomas Holopainen)

'Sleeping Sun' is an undisputed Nightwish classic and it's hard to think of *Oceanborn* without it following its late inclusion on Drakkar versions of the album and all subsequent editions. A refreshingly accessible power ballad, it proves that Nightwish are more than capable of delivering chart-bothering anthems should the need arise.

And the need did arise, courtesy of Drakkar records, who requested a new song to promote in Germany to coincide with the solar eclipse of 1999. The aptly named maxi single *Sleeping Sun (Four Ballads of the Eclipse)* comprised the made-to-order new track, 'Walking in the Air', 'Swanheart' and the title track from *Angels Fall First*. Whilst not a huge commercial success, Drakkar credit the song with bringing significant exposure to the group and improving sales of *Oceanborn* across Germany. A winning venture it may have been for the record label, but Tuomas emphatically requested that he never be asked to pen a single song in such a way ever again.

'Sleeping Sun' seemed determined to be a thorn in Tuomas' side as it was re-recorded in 2005 as the group's last song with Tarja. In support of the *Highest Hopes*: *The Best of Nightwish* compilation, the remake was prompted by Tarja's desire to update her vocals, something Tuomas and Emppu both considered deeply unnecessary. Tarja's persistence won over and the band took the opportunity to re-record with bassist Marco (and thus assign him some royalties from the song) and a loss of the original keyboard recordings meant Tuomas himself was also tasked with recapturing the magic of the song 16 years later.

If nothing else, the 2005 remake offered the band the chance to right the wrongs of the music video. The original clip featured a serene Tarja standing before the striking backdrop of Inari, Finland and, for some unknown reason, emerging from a bathtub in the middle of a field. The new cut, directed by Joern Heitmann, cast the group as knights on a vicious battlefield as Tarja sauntered through in an angelic white gown. It wasn't a logical visual for a song about an eclipse, but it earned the plaudit of the band's best video of their career to date from the ever-critical Tuomas.

Deceptively tricky to perform, Floor Jansen commented to *Tuonela* magazine that 'Sleeping Sun' is 'only beautiful when it's sung perfectly. You can't be off with it. The dynamics, everything needs to be there'. Despite the challenge, all of the band's lead vocalists have performed 'Sleeping Sun', underlining its remarkable staying power across setlists from the *Oceanborn* era right through to the group's virtual shows in support of *Human. :||: Nature.*

'Nightquest' 4:17 (Music and lyrics: Tuomas Holopainen)
A clear bedfellow with *Angels Fall First*'s 'Elvenpath', 'Nightquest' is a fantastical romp that just felt too naïve to make the album's final cut. Lyrically, the song is self-referencing as it serves as a mission statement of the young Finns; 'Led by a maid, Queen of the night' nods to Tarja whilst 'the wanderer, storyteller' refers to Tuomas, our 'merry minstrel' is Emppu and the 'hammerheart' is Jukka on drums. Prophesising *Oceanborn*'s unexpected success, the group invite 'legions of night-time wanderers' to follow their pied piper tunes and declare a patriotism to a land of 'neverwaking dream'.

All in all, yes, 'Nightquest' is a bit silly, even more so when taken in the context of the more mature *Oceanborn* record, but there is a charm to its excitable nature and a celebration of the purity and innocence that Tuomas would later come to yearn for.

Wishmaster (2000)

Personnel:
Emppu Vuorinen: guitars
Sami Vänskä: bass
Tarja Turunen: vocals
Jukka Nevalainen: drums, percussions
Tuomas Holopainen: synthesizers
Sam Hardwick: spoken word ('Dead Boy's Poem')
Ike Vil: spoken word ('The Kinslayer')
Esa Lehtinen: Flute
Matias Kaila: tenor vocals
Kimmo Kallio: baritone vocals
Riku Salminen: bass vocals
Anssi Honkanen: bass vocals
Ville Laaksonen: tenor vocals, choir arrangements
Recorded and engineered by Tero Kinnunen at Caverock studio and Mikko Karmila at Finnvox Studios
Recorded between January and March 2000
Produced and arranged by Nightwish and Tero Kinnunen
Mika Jussila: mastering
Mikko Karmila: mixing
Toni Härkönen: band photography
Markus Mayer: cover art
Maria Sandell: inlay art

According to Tuomas, the band's third opus *Wishmaster* 'mostly just corrected *Oceanborn*'s mistakes' and whilst it may not have been as transformative as the band's other album eras, save for birthing a comedy viral smash in Fishmaster, the record is just as fundamental in their trajectory. Upgrading from Finnish sports halls, the band brought the album together in Finnvox Studios and, compared to the struggles of *Oceanborn*, the sessions went swimmingly. That was until the band spotted pirates in the waves.

The music industry was more than a decade away from the dominance of streaming and quite how the internet would coexist with physical media was yet to be established. *Wishmaster* became the band's first real victim of piracy and whilst it caused a wave of frustration amongst the camp, it was underlined with a realisation: there was real demand building for a new Nightwish record.

When *Wishmaster* dropped, a few weeks earlier than scheduled due to the internet leaks, it couldn't have done much better in their homeland, reaching number one in the Finnish album charts and receiving rave reviews. The promotion from Drakkar also helped secure a peak at number 21 in Germany and even made a dent in France.

Whilst Tuomas considered the sessions a breeze, Tarja had an altogether different recollection of the *Wishmaster* recordings as she discussed with *Metal Rules*:

> We had been touring like hell for that album [*Oceanborn*], got very exhausted from touring and even got tired of seeing each other's faces at that time... this was culminated pretty heavily into the recording of *Wishmaster*, the mother of all our troubles that we channelled right into the stressful studio sessions of this particular album. We kind of managed to get rid of our shitty feelings right after we had finished the recordings for *Wishmaster,* and because of that, it was much easier and more comfortable for us to start doing gigs again. Because of our somewhat shitty feelings during the recording sessions of *Wishmaster*, it turned out be to a damn dark and even scary album, both musically and lyrically in my opinion.

Perhaps a reflection of the focus on refinement rather than reinvention, musically, *Wishmaster* doesn't make any huge leaps away from the sounds explored on its predecessor. The power metal sound continues to underpin the album's heavier moments ('Crownless', 'Wanderlust') but is juxtaposed with some of their most sparse arrangements to date ('Two for Tragedy', 'Deep Silent Complete').

You would be forgiven for expecting the album to be a particularly poignant work for Holopainen, if only due to the inclusion of the heart-wrenching ballad 'Dead Boy's Poem', something he himself labelled 'the mother of all Nightwish songs'. Reflecting on the album for the Spinefarm Reloaded re-release, Tuomas commented:

> 'Dead Boy's Poem' took on a life of its own, becoming a kind of symbol for Nightwish's identity as a band. Despite this, however, *Wishmaster* is the most distant and least personal album in the Nightwish catalogue. You could say that it continues the fantasy trip started on ***Oceanborn***, ranging from the real-life tragedy of 'The Kinslayer', through to the lovers' tale of 'Come Cover Me' and on to the massive Disney feast of 'FantasMic'.

Wishmaster was the pinnacle of the band's power metal years and garnered acclaim for fan favourite hits such as the title track and opening gambit 'She Is My Sin'. A testament to its success, years later, enthusiasts still yearn for a return to the more complex, frantic guitar work that characterised the band's earlier work, and the charismatic guitarist Emppu Vuorinen certainly paid his dues during the era, carrying the weight of many tracks. As later albums would see guitar solos slowly wind down to a rarity, *Wishmaster* remains the golden years for fans of Emppu's playing and his most front-and-centre contributions to the Nightwish story.

Keen to build on their success and expand into new European markets, Nightwish decided to throw their hat into the Eurovision ring. With the song 'Sleepwalker', a slightly more ambient sound than their usual power metal leanings, they entered the Finnish selection show but were ultimately pipped to the post by Nina Åström. The band needn't have worried. If *Wishmaster* was more of a plateau, it was to serve only as a brief moment of calm before the enormity of the sound and success that was on the horizon.

'She is My Sin' 4:46 (Music and lyrics: Tuomas Holopainen)
It is criminal that 'She Is My Sin' was never released as a single, such has been its lasting legacy ever since the release of *Wishmaster*. The sinister burst of synths that open the track find their rightful place at the start of the record, an attention-grabbing invitation into the power-metal onslaught that makes up the first two tracks and a good chunk of the record as a whole. Lyrically, the song once again leans on religious metaphors as a lustful longing, deliciously tempting and forbidden, is dangled before Tuomas.

'She Is My Sin' has been a setlist mainstay, outlasting most of its album-mates when it came to future tour considerations. As such, the song can be heard on the *From Wishes to Eternity* release and both live releases with Floor Jansen at the helm – *Showtime, Storytime* and *Vehicle of Spirit*. Whilst it has earned its merit on the live circuit, the song is a peculiar omission from the band's *Highest Hopes: The Best of Nightwish* and *Decades* compilations, though the former did tack on a live performance on the bonus DVD.

Speaking of Ms Jansen, years before joining Nightwish and whilst still performing with the Dutch metallers After Forever, the group covered 'She Is My Sin' during numerous live performances. Little did Floor know that she'd later become the frontwoman of the very band they were playing tribute to.

'The Kinslayer' 3:59 (Music and lyrics: Tuomas Holopainen)
Drifting away from religious allusions and fantasy worlds, 'The Kinslayer' is a song inspired by the 1999 Columbine Massacre and firmly rooted Nightwish in the present day. Musically, it upped the tension with a guest contribution from Babylon Whores vocalist Ike Vil as a taunting, effective duet partner to Tarja.

The Columbine High School Massacre was a highly publicised shooting in Colorado, US in which twelve students and one teacher were murdered by gunmen Eric Harris and Dylan Klebold, who were also students at the school. 'The Kinslayer' draws closely on the reports from the attack, which informed the lyrics – Tuomas explained on the band's official site:

> They [Harris and Klebold] had no real motive. They made a videotape in the morning just before the massacre where they said: 'We are going to kill you all. You have been giving us shit for years. We want to say

> our sorry for our parents; there's nothing you could have done. This is something we must do. We're sorry; we didn't like life very much...' The event is something I will never understand. If something as horrible as this can happen in this world, there's no sense, no truth to cling to anymore. I find there's a great deal of symbolism hidden in this happening. The dialogue in the middle of the song quotes the actual phrases between the killers and their schoolmates during the shooting, according to those who survived.

It was a brave step outside of the band's usual muses and was a timely reflection on the tragic event. As such, the song was used as a promotional single for *Wishmaster* and was one of only two of the album's tracks that were included on the *Decades* compilation, as curated by Tuomas himself. The song would also be included in the subsequent tour, though was erroneously titled on the *Decades: Live in Buenos Aires* live DVD and Blu-ray tracklists as 'The Kingslayer'.

'Come Cover Me' 4:34 (Music: Tuomas Holopainen, Emppu Vuorinen, lyrics: Tuomas Holopainen)
Another track included on the *Decades* tour, 'Come Cover Me', is a comparatively gentler affair following the impact of the first two tracks. The midtempo song has a simple premise of young love, so whom better to draw upon for its lyrics than William Shakespeare? From Sonnet 9 ('Is it for fear to wet a widow's eye') to Sonnet 34 ('To dry the rain on my storm-beaten face'), the playwright is a firm influence whilst Tarja's counterpart in the romantic dance is Emppu's melodic guitar lines, proving to be just as infectious as the vocal lines.

When it came time to resurrect the song for the live set in 2018, Tarja was no longer a part of the group, but Floor Jansen was not tasked with going it alone, thanks to co-vocalists Troy Donockley and Marco Hietala. Troy discussed with *Metal Blast*:

> On this *Decades* tour, there are a lot more backing vocals. We've gone seriously into harmony vocals, which is really a delight. It really transformed songs like 'Come Cover Me', which we sing in a three-part harmony. Also, I'm playing harmony guitars to Emppu, which is a nice development, since I can now fill out the underground while he solos on the top with rhythm and things like that.

'Wanderlust' 4:49 (Music and lyrics: Tuomas Holopainen)
After pondering life's questions on 'Know Where the Nightingale Sings', 'Wanderlust' takes the inquisitive Holopainen through to the logical next step – a thirst for experience and to be a part of the awe he was keenly witnessing. If *Oceanborn* was a chance for him to make music his sole

ncome, it was on *Wishmaster* that he dared to ponder what might have been. Describing the song on the official Nightwish site, he shared:

> It's a cliché that life's one big journey. But that's the way it is. And there's so much to discover and experience on this planet. I couldn't bear the thought that I would have to live my life with the biggest experience being a one-week trip to the Canary Islands after working in an office for one year straight. Routine kills everything. I wish people would find the 'wanderer within'.

An unquenchable inner curiosity may be the impetus, but it's also a fitting tribute to the significant increase in touring that the group embarked on in support of their second record; across 33 dates in Finland and further 26 in Europe, Nightwish were beginning to practice the very wanderlust that they preached.

'Two for Tragedy' 3:50 (Music and lyrics: Tuomas Holopainen)
The heart-wrenching ballad 'Two for Tragedy' remains an enigma in the Nightwish catalogue, with precious few mentions of it across interviews and no live performances to speak of. The curiosity is amplified by the nature of the song, which demands attention from the off with its sparse opening verse and a profoundly moving performance from Tarja.

It's with Turunen that the song did eventually make its live debut, as part of her solo performance in 2006 alongside the Savonlinna orchestra and choir. As for the composer? He leaves us only with the succinct comment, 'the biggest tragedies always require two...'

'Wishmaster' 4:23 (Music and lyrics: Tuomas Holopainen)
It would be years later that Nightwish truly (and consciously) dominated YouTube audiences with 'Ghost Love Score', but their first taste of viral success came via the album's title track which birthed a misheard lyrics video uploaded in 2006; 'Fishmaster' transformed the song into an ode to hamsters, dentists, hard porn, and Steven Seagull and racked up an impressive 13 and a half million views.

The actual song was less concerned with dentistry and rodents, instead serving as another nod towards Tuomas' keen interest in fantasy, particularly his personal favourites J.R.R Tolkien and '80s franchise *Dragonlance*. It felt less serious than many other tracks on the album, particularly the puncturing 'Two for Tragedy' which had preceded it, yet it never feels as naïve as its thematic bedfellow 'Elvenpath', demonstrating an evident growth in Tuomas' songwriting.

'Wishmaster' also serves as a galvanising wake-up call for anyone sitting by idly and waiting for their dreams and aspirations to come true – Tuomas shared as much on the band's official site: 'We are the masters of our own wishes, beliefs and dreams. Whatever you desire enough, it can happen. Destiny is an excuse for those who don't have the strength to fulfil their wishes. Everything is possible. Even the impossible'. 'Wishmaster' was the perfect soundtrack to such a demand, offering up the band's most epic, chant-along chorus to date – all the bombast conjured without even a sniff of an orchestra.

'Bare Grace Misery' 3:39 (Music: Tuomas Holopainen, Emppu Vuorinen, lyrics: Tuomas Holopainen)

Whether it was the fracas between Tuomas and Emppu during the *Oceanborn* recording sessions or the success of his sole *Oceanborn* contribution 'Sacrament of Wilderness', Emppu Vuorinen was credited with contributions to three *Wishmaster* tracks: 'Come Cover Me', 'Crownless' and 'Bare Grace Misery'. Naturally, the guitar is prominent across all three, but this effort also demonstrated a knack for drawing it back when needed, perfectly underscoring Tarja's layered vocals.

Whilst 'She Is My Sin' was told from the perspective of the tempted, it's the temptress that we hear from in 'Bare Grace Misery'. An almost Bathory figure, though thirsty for innocence and purity rather than beauty, the femme fatale seems resigned to her unrepentant life of sin. The song references Lucrece, a Shakespearean character that was left suicidal after being raped. Could it be that the seductress is the devastated Lucrece seeking her revenge?

'Crownless' 4:26 (Music: Tuomas Holopainen, Emppu Vuorinen, lyrics: Tuomas Holopainen)

If 'Bare Grace Misery' found Emppu holding back, he fully unleashes on the power metal riot that is 'Crownless'. The intense, ferocious guitar hits from the start and remains incessant throughout the entire song, mischievously daring Tarja to keep up. At the midway point, a roguish battle between Tuomas' synths and Emppu's guitar solo breaks out before the song resets, stripping back to that opening riff all over again.

Tarja confessed to *Whiplash* that she was not so keen on the song: 'I'm definitely not proud to have sung it… it's a lot of power metal, it sounds too cliche, I guess. It doesn't work, I didn't fit'. For Tuomas, however, it was a necessary outlet of irritation, sharing the following summary of 'Crownless' on Nightwish's site:

> Arrogant, egotistic people make me sick! Those people who have been given a crown but can't carry it properly. Nothing is everlasting and the fall can be very sudden. I think we all should keep that in mind and be proud of the things we have achieved in a positive way.

In amongst the excitement, 'Crownless' also signals to *Oceanborn* track 'The Riddler' as Tuomas adulates the humble over those sitting atop their own self-built pedestals.

'Deep Silent Complete' 3:57 (Music and lyrics: Tuomas Holopainen)
Another consistent theme across Nightwish albums is the majesty of the oceans; from *Oceanborn* to the devil in the deep and ocean soul, a title Tuomas bestows upon himself across the *Wishmaster* album and a sustained motif in its follow-up *Century Child*.

'Deep Silent Complete' is a tribute to the seas and marvels at the power of the formidable waters, a lush arrangement mimicking the siren song that Tarja sings of. The song draws yet again on Shakespeare's sonnets, specifically 'The age to come would say 'This poet lies; such heavenly touches ne'er touched earthly faces'' from Sonnet 17 and 'But heaven in thy creation did decree that in thy face sweet love should ever dwell' from Sonnet 93. Instead of singing his adoration to a lover, however, it's the big blue expanse which Tuomas repurposes Shakespeare's words to honour.

With 'Wishmaster' and 'She Is My Sin' as enduring classics from the album, 'Deep Silent Complete' feels an odd pick for the first (and only) official single, albeit without a promotional video. It is one of the most serene album cuts and is certainly not reflective of the wider power metal sound that governed the record as a whole. Not quite managing to topple the success of 'Sacrament of Wilderness', 'Deep Silent Complete' did manage to peak at number 3 in the Finnish charts and was later certified gold for surpassing 5000 sales.

'Dead Boy's Poem' 6:47 (Music and lyrics: Tuomas Holopainen)
The aforementioned ocean soul gets its first nod in the band's history on 'Dead Boy's Poem', an appropriate introduction to the recurrent moniker as Tuomas declared the song an extremely personal account of what he considers to be his lasting legacy. Tuomas revealed as much on the official Nightwish site when discussing the *Wishmaster* tracks:

> This is the most personal song I've ever written. My testimony for the whole world. With this song, I want to apologise to everyone who deserves my apology. It also makes an 'I don't care' statement to them who deserve it. The song is also about what Nightwish means and has meant to me. It's all, without it I'm dead. I have created it and it has created me. When I pass away, this song's lyrics are of what I wish to be remembered. An Ocean Soul.

Coined at the time as 'the mother of all Nightwish songs', it's easy to see why. Yet again, it breaks from the metallic side of *Wishmaster* in a similar way to 'Two for Tragedy', but whilst that song had been structurally more familiar, 'Dead Boy's Poem' stretches out to almost seven minutes and allows itself to segue into spoken word elements and fade out to a tranquil recitation.

Sam Hardwick, the young boy playing the role of the dead boy, was drafted in thanks to some familial connections, as Tuomas explained in the band's biography:

> I had an idea of a song with a young boy reciting a poem … the trouble was that no Finnish twelve-year-old could pronounce English right, so I had to find a native speaker. My mother's sister, actress Miitta Sorvali, knew the English-Finnish director and writer Neil Hardwick well, and my mom remembered that Neil had a son called Sam. I called him and asked him to do the poem, and Sam agreed right away. It was just funny that when I talked to this fifteen-year-old boy, he seemed like such a citizen of the world, and was actually familiar with our band. Sam said he'd be free to record the poem anytime, I just had to give him a call. He even knew where Finnvox was and promised to meet us there… I gave him the poem, and he read it through a few times. We did some editing, and Sam just sat down on the studio floor and read his book, after which I asked him to read the poem a couple more times.

Clearly leaving an impact on the band, Hardwick would return to bookend the next album *Century Child*, reprising his role as the narrative dead boy.

'FantasMic' 8:18 (Music and lyrics: Tuomas Holopainen)
It's an unenviable task having to follow up the impactful 'Dead Boy's Poem', but 'FantasMic' was just enough of a thematic contrast to successfully end the album on a note of earnest fun. It once again strayed away from a predictable structure and was comprised of three parts – unlike 'Lappi' on *Angels Fall First*, all three are consolidated into one track on the record – the third of which being incorporated into live sets following *Wishmaster*'s release.

Prepare your Disney bingo card as the song salutes the animation company's most influential works at a rapid pace, including *Fantasia*, *Snow White*, *The Little Mermaid*, *Beauty and the Beast*, *The Lion King* and *Mulan* to name just a few. The mention of White Agony Creek points towards the character of Scrooge McDuck, for whom Tuomas would compose his first solo album, *Music Inspired by the Life and Times of Scrooge,* boasting a cover created by Scrooge McDuck's original cartoonist Don Rosa.

As the unabating 'wish upon a star' hook reprises to form the album's closing burst of bombast, many will argue that the record's grand finale is somewhat overshadowed by the indelible 'Dead Boy's Poem' that came before it. And whilst this may prove true when reviewing Nightwish's legacy in hindsight, it's hard to envision anything else closing out the triumphant power metal of *Wishmaster* with quite as much vigour and spirit as 'FantasMic'. This fist-in-the-air peak that concludes the album finds Nightwish on an apex of achievement, joyously unaware that an imposing emotional plummet would come to define *Wishmaster*'s eventual successor

'Sleepwalker' 2:57 (Music and lyrics: Tuomas Holopainen)
Intended as a slightly different take on their signature sound, 'Sleepwalker' was Nightwish's stab at representing Finland in the Eurovision Song Contest.

It dialled down Tarja's soaring voice and restrained the heavier side of the band to deliver a more ambient, atmospheric effort with the hopes of being more digestible by the masses. One could argue that this was where it went wrong as the group were pipped to the post by Nina Åström and her track 'A Little Bit', but that would be to discredit the massive 38% of televotes that the band secured, almost twice as many as Åström, landing them in third place after being tanked by the professional juries. The group were not disheartened, least of all Tarja, who was frank about her opposition to competing in the contest in the first place, Tuomas later admitting that their entire involvement was an attempt to shake up the more conservative side of the Finnish music scene.

'Sleepwalker' had been produced alongside Merv de Peyer upon the record label's suggestion. De Peyer also brought in the electronic elements rarely heard in a Nightwish track, though Tuomas later admitted to *Metal Rules* that 'the production for it was kind of so-so and in my opinion, it's the worst sounding Nightwish song we have ever done'. A 'heavy version' was produced, a little more in-keeping with the band's style though still a clear outlier on the *Wishmaster* editions it would later be tacked onto. Speaking to *Metal Hammer*, Tuomas explained the reason for the different versions:

> The regular CD version of this number wouldn't have gone through [to Eurovision], so we recorded two versions of 'Sleepwalker', one, especially for this festival. It was placed on a single and we recorded it in London under the watchful eye of Merv de Peyer. It doesn't sound so hard because we cut off some of the lines, but it kept the atmosphere of our compositions. The one on *Wishmaster* is much heavier.

Far from being ousted, however, 'Sleepwalker' was included as a B-side on the single release of 'Deep Silent Complete' and featured on the *Bless the Child* EP years later. Its chorus was also extracted to form the title of the band's first documentary DVD *End of Innocence*.

Over The Hills and Far Away (2001)

Personnel:
Tarja Turunen: vocals
Tuomas Holopainen: keyboards, mixing, backing vocals ('Over the Hills and Far Away')
Emppu Vuorinen: guitars
Sami Vänskä: bass guitar, cover photo (Spinefarm version)
Jukka Nevalainen: drums
Tony Kakko: vocals ('Astral Romance'), backing vocals ('Over The Hills and Far Away')
Tapio Wilska: vocals ('10th Man Down')
Recorded by Tero Kinnunen and Mikko Karmila at Caverock and Finnvox studios
Recorded between February and March 2001
Arranged by Tuomas Holopainen and Tero Kinnunen (except 'Over The Hills and Far Away' by Gary Moore)
Mixed by Mikko Karmila, Tero Kinnunen and Tuomas Holopainen at Finnvox Studio in March 2001
Mika Jussila: mastering
Håkon Grav, Hasse Sukis, Timo Isoaho: photography (Spinefarm version)
Jan Carlsson, Mikko Joona, Marcelo Rossi: photography (Drakkar version)
Peter Dell: cover photo (Drakkar version)

My, how the times have changed. As plans were readied for *Wishmaster*'s follow-up, a two-year timeframe for the group to write, record and release a new record was considered far too long. Laughable as this may be, with four and five-year gaps as standard these days, the band wisely wanted to keep up the momentum of their growing fanbase and international interest. *From Wishes to Eternity*, the band's first live DVD/CD was a huge success, but it was a thirst for new material that proved the foundation of the *Over The Hills and Far Away* EP.

Eventually, the four tracks included a couple of new recordings and a pair of nearly-news as well as a wealth of tacked-on live tracks taken from the *From Wishes to Eternity* release that had preceded it a few months earlier. Tarja explained the release to *Rock Brigade* in 2001:

> Well, our last album, *Wishmaster,* was released in May of last year. Already at that time, we knew that the next album would take more time to be done, so we would have to offer something to the fans in the meantime. That was the main reason we did this expanded EP, which in Finland, by the way, is only a single of four songs. In the other countries, there are the live tracks. It's kind of a complicated thing, there were a lot of versions of it out there. Anyway, we needed to give something new to our fans while the next album was not released. 'Over The Hills and Far Away' is a nice song, though it's nothing special, but we all like it. It was Tuomas' idea to make

this song. He likes it a lot, so we didn't intend to do much more than Gary Moore had already done in his version.

As with *Wishmaster*, the EP wasn't a particularly personal venture for Tuomas and is not reflected upon too kindly in either the biography or even in interviews promoting the release. Despite this, it birthed a cover version that would become a setlist mainstay and, thanks to its live track inclusions, served as an enjoyable glance back at the band's journey so far.

'Over The Hills and Far Away' 5:03 (Music and lyrics: Gary Moore)
If there was any fear that domestic interest was waning, 'Over the Hills and Far Away' rescinded any doubts. Voted by the *Soundi* poll as the Finnish song of the year, what had initially been tucked away on a between-album EP ended up being one of the band's biggest hits; once again hitting the top spot in Finland, the track remained in the charts for a whopping 49 weeks and was certified platinum.

The visual drought of *Wishmaster* was drawn to a close with not only the entire *From Wishes to Eternity* release, but also a decent video for the EP's lead single. Filmed at the Suomenlinna Maritime Fortress just off Helsinki, the band look every bit the confident professionals, a world away from the sheepish youngsters shown on the 'Sacrament of Wilderness' clip. No doubt, the visual accompaniment helped prolong the success of the track as videos became ever more important during the new millennium – a relief too, that the latest one doing the rounds finally matched the quality of the group's music.

'Over The Hills and Far Away' might not have been an obvious cover choice but a deep love for the track within the band prompted its selection and despite her dismissal of it to *Rock Brigade*, Tarja went on to tell Tiefgang Online:

> We love this song. It has everything a metal song needs, beautiful melodies, a lot of drive, a lot of power and it offers a lot of space to experiment. Somehow it was clear that we wanted to record a cover, but nobody really knew anything. When the name of this song came up, everyone was immediately thrilled. I know that it sounds strange to hear this song with my voice because it is normally written and sung by Gary Moore himself, you can't imagine a singer to match it. But I had a lot of fun singing this song.

There was a nostalgic pull for Tuomas, too, who admitted to Solemn Music that the song was 'one of the first I heard when I was a kid that I really liked'. A young Holopainen would have been forgiven for missing the bittersweet story of 'Over The Hills and Far Away' at the time; it tells of a man, wrongfully accused of a crime, who is unable to confess his innocence as his alibi would oust a sensitive secret – that he spent the evening with the wife of his best friend.

Gary Moore's original had also been a hit in Finland, reaching number one in the Finnish charts in January 1987, however, the songwriter was not exactly gushing when it came time to survey the resurgence of his hit, as he spoke to *Classic Rock*:

> To me, it had a bit of a karaoke vibe because the backing track was so similar. I don't mean that insultingly, but it was almost identical. I believe they're a pretty big band now, so it's cool that they did it.

'10th Man Down' 5:20 (Music and lyrics: Tuomas Holopainen)
Time has been kind to '10th Man Down'. Whilst it may initially have been overshadowed by the enormous success of 'Over The Hills and Far Away', this fierce cut laid in wait for any keen Nightwish listeners happening upon it. Of the three new tracks included on the EP, it's undoubtedly the strongest and much more closely tied to the more dramatic leanings of *Wishmaster* and *Oceanborn*.

Tapio Wilska returns on guest vocals and contrasts excellently with Tarja as the two lament the trauma of war; in Tarja, we have a howling desperation and in Tapio, a miserable suffering. '10th Man Down' tells the story of a troubled soldier envying the deaths of those he had killed, realising that they had managed to escape the ceaseless torment of a life after war. It's an uncomfortable listen at times, an honest and passionate plea from Holopainen who later discussed his time in the Finnish army with *Metal Hammer*:

> I absolutely detested it, but it's mandatory in Finland that all the males go to the army. You can stay there for six or nine months or go to the civil service, which takes at least 12 months. I decided to take the short path and try my luck entering the military band. You had to do all the shit with the guns and all that for eight weeks, but luckily I spent the next seven months playing about 300 shows and marches with the band. I would have lost my mind [if they sent me to the warzone] because I can't handle guns. I hate them more than anything. I believe in self-defence, so I'm not a pacifist in that sense. I'm just very anti-gun, except for sport and hunting.

Though the EP's title track had a lengthy moment in the sun during Tarja's era with Nightwish, it was with Floor that '10th Man Down' went some way in challenging it for long-awaited adoration. It was lifted from the vaults for inclusion on the *Decades* tour setlist and, for many fans, proved to be a blinding highlight with its refreshed production and winning performances from both Floor and Marco. Perhaps the deciding blow between this underrated gem and 'Over The Hills and Far Away' was the *Decades* tracklist compiled by Tuomas – containing only one contribution from the EP, it was '10th Man Down' that was justifiably chosen for inclusion.

'Away' 4:32 (Music and lyrics: Tuomas Holopainen)
If 'Over The Hills and Far Away' and '10th Man Down' were sparring for the title of EP highlight, poor 'Away' never stood a chance. Even in early promotional interviews, it was swept under the carpet, Tarja admitting that it wouldn't be included in setlists and Tuomas refraining from mentioning it at all in the Spinefarm reloaded re-release. The ballad received a final nail in the coffin when *Once Upon a Nightwish* was published in which the songwriter labelled it 'a whopping piece of crap'.

Ever self-critical, perhaps Tuomas' remarks are a little harsh. 'Away' is certainly not a Nightwish standout, but it can boast some magical arrangements in the verse and a decent, if forgettable, chorus. The record label ran with a tweaked lyric from the song as they emblazoned 'every wish is only a journey away' on the back of the hugely successful *From Wishes to Eternity* DVD. 'Away' itself, however, had precious little chance of being considered for the setlist and has never been performed (nor mentioned) since.

'Astral Romance (Remake 2001)' 5:18 (Music and lyrics: Tuomas Holopainen)
Keen to distance themselves from Tuomas' questionable vocals on the band's debut, by the time *From Wishes to Eternity* was recorded, songs featuring Tuomas' voice were either cut from the set or reinterpreted with a more capable guest vocalist. 'Astral Romance' became the one track immortalised in a studio remake, this time featuring Tony Kakko, who had also helped transform 'Beauty and the Beast' live and was well known for his work with the power metal Finns Sonata Arctica.

The two bands remained close, their histories interlinked thanks to a firm friendship between Tuomas and Tony. Future collaborations included numerous support slots from Sonata Arctica, guest appearances during Nightwish sets (Tony returned to the stage with the group for performances of 'The Islander' and 'Last Ride of the Day' at Rock in Rio 2015) and Tony's collaboration with Tuomas on his solo album. Kakko also made the most of his trip to the studio, providing backing vocals for the EP's title track.

Although Holopainen reflected that the remake of 'Astral Romance' seemed 'forced', it felt fair to re-present the song to Nightwish's growing audience. Anyone dismissing *Angels Fall First* as a comparative slog compared to the more concise *Oceanborn* and *Wishmaster* may have missed the few gems hidden amongst its tracklist. It's no mystery as to why 'Beauty and the Beast' and 'Elvenpath' remained two of the only tracks incorporated into live sets from *Wishmaster* onwards, but despite its necessity for a male vocalist, 'Astral Romance' deserves to be counted amongst the debut's standout offerings.

'Kiteen Pallo' 1:09 (Music: Nightwish)
Clocking in at just over a minute, the short instrumental had a dual purpose as the galvanising entrance music of Kitee's sports team Kiteen Pallo and as

the soundtrack to the documentary DVD *End of Innocence*. Pesäpallo, the team's sport, is considered by many as the national sport of Finland and has similarities to baseball and rounders. Ahead of the release of *Imaginaerum*, Nightwish offered up another composition for the team – this time lifting elements of the then-unreleased 'Last Ride of the Day' as remixed by Finnish DJ Tapio Hakanen (DJ Orkidea), who went on to give an extended dance overhaul to Nightwish's 2008 single 'Bye Bye Beautiful'.

Century Child (2002)

Personnel:
Tarja Turunen: vocals
Tuomas Holopainen: keys, piano
Emppu Vuorinen: guitars
Marco Hietala: bass, vocals
Jukka Nevalainen: drums
Joensuu City Orchestra: orchestra
Juha Ikonen: orchestra leader
Riku Niemi: orchestra and choir conductor, arranger and producer
Mongo Aaltonen: orchestral percussion
Hilkka Kangasniemi: choirmaster
Sam Hardwick: spoken word ('Bless The Child', 'Beauty of the Beast')
Kristiina Ilmonen: tin whistle ('Forever Yours')
GME choir: additional möykkä (noise)
Terhi Kallio: orchestra engineering
Recorded by Tero Kinnunen and Mikko Karmila at Caverock and Finnvox studios
Recorded between January and March 2002
Arranged by Tuomas Holopainen and Tero Kinnunen
Mixed by Mikko Karmila, Tero Kinnunen and Tuomas Holopainen at Finnvox Studio in April 2002
Produced by Tuomas Holopainen and Tero Kinnunen
Co-produced by Nightwish
Mika Jussila: mastering
Toni Härkönen: band photography
Markus Mayer: cover art

For a time, *Century Child* was to serve as the final Nightwish album. Tarja had given warning that it would be her last record with the band, a decision made clearer by declining communication between the band members even if a return to the classical genre was cited as her official reason. This rift appeared to stem from Turunen's hiring of future husband Marcelo Cabuli as her own manager, whilst Ewo Pohjola served as the Nightwish band manager. Intended to help the band focus solely on the music, it aided only in widening the chasm between the members. But these tensions were to fester a little longer yet, with bassist Sami Vänskä serving as the sacrificial offering required to give the band a much-needed rebirth.

Century Child established itself as the band's most formative record to date. Perhaps the most crucial difference between this album and the releases before it was the move away from power metal and firmly into the world of symphonic metal. Orchestral elements, bombastic crescendos and a multi-part epic began to build the template for what would become the signature Nightwish sound. The inherent drama also felt like a natural fit for Tarja's operatic vocals, which had gone from strength to strength through the years, something many may not have expected from over half a decade of exposure in the metal sphere.

The album's widened scope was signified by Tuomas in an interview with *Metal Brasil*:

> I like to try new things on every album. I want to try new styles still within our sound. It's not the intention to completely change styles like Metallica and Paradise Lost did, but I always try to include new elements. This experience with the orchestra was something I always wanted to do. Nightwish songs are very orchestral, with choirs and everything. I've always used the keyboards to create this atmosphere and this time, I made sure to see what it would be like with a real orchestra. It was a splendid surprise: the orchestra did a very good job and matched a lot with the band. It was the hardest album to make, for sure.

It may not be the most 'metal' approach, but the band were quickly learning that a level of professionalism was required at this stage of their career and, whilst not nearly as publicised as the band's vocalist firings, the split with Sami Vänskä weighed heavily on the composition of the record. Frustrations began to build as Vänskä repeatedly turned up late to meetings and showed little enthusiasm onstage – he would later confess to growing bored of the endless touring – resulting in Ewo Pohjola, fresh into his role as Nightwish band manager, having to deliver the news that he had been dismissed. The ousting of a friend, however, had a huge impact on Tuomas, as he recalled in the Spinefarm reloaded re-release:

> A musician's work is always a mirror of his personal life. Sometimes it's so revealing, it can be scary. By the time I got to writing *Century Child*, days of happiness were well and truly over, making it the darkest album in the band's history to date. It's also the only one of our records that follows some kind of theme; *Century Child* is a dumping ground for the emotions, a defence mechanism against the world, from the dead end of 'Slaying the Dreamer' through to the hopelessness of 'Ocean Soul', although 'Ever Dream' hints at the promise of light at the end of the tunnel.

Inviting Marco Hietala into the fold as the replacement for Vänskä, turned out to be a serendipitous decision; Marco played a significant role in Nightwish's transforming sound, introducing male vocals to the mix and providing a charismatic stage presence on tour. Whether from Sami's exit or Marco's inherent warmth, the new bassist noted that the troupe began to feel a 'solidarity and togetherness' as they began their promotional activities and subsequent tours. Indeed, even Tarja remained a part of the group for another album despite her intention to wrap things up with Nightwish.

Whilst not a concept album as such, the lyrics on *Century Child* proved to be another Nightwish cornerstone as Tuomas yearned for the loss of youthful innocence, a theme he'd return to time and again. Bookended by an emotional return from *Wishmaster*'s 'dead boy' Sam Hardwick, *Century Child* was a masterful juxtaposition of sombre and bleak reflections against enormous soundscapes. Behind the scenes, they may have been scrambling to stay united but to the outside world, Nightwish were confidently levelling up.

'Bless The Child' 6:12 (Music and lyrics: Tuomas Holopainen)
The first song composed for *Century Child* also ended up as the opening track. The pulsating introduction fading up from silence already took a clear step away from the electrifying openers of *Wishmaster* and *Oceanborn*. Considering the spellbinding impact the orchestral elements had across the album, it was no coincidence either that one of the tracks featuring the Joensuu City Orchestra was given the task of opening proceedings, transforming and solidifying Nightwish's signature sound. A particularly beloved composer was the inspiration as Tuomas told Perkele magazine 'Hans Zimmer's influence can be heard and the song follows well this soundtrack line, in the line of the movie *Gladiator*. The lyrics clarify the theme of the whole album'.

'Bless The Child' continued the trend of enhanced music videos, though the interspersed storyline ends up a little muddled and confusing. Telling the story of a romance in reverse, a grieving partner turns to alcohol before the narrative flows back to his marriage and eventually his meeting his future wife as children. Is the message that their love helped them rediscover a purity they had lost? Were they in heaven at the end? Of visual quality, a little muddled thematically. It was also a strange choice to dwindle the encompassing theme of lost innocence into what appeared to be a standard love story, though the band shots remained effective as the group leaned into their gothic image to support the album's more macabre concerns.

Alongside 'Ever Dream', the song had a lasting impact on setlists and appeared on all subsequent tours with the exception of the *Decades* retrospective and *Dark Passion Play* venture. The physical release was also a treasure trove for Nightwish diehards as the *Bless the Child* EP compiled many rarities and bonus tracks from previous eras, the Spinefarm and Drakkar single versions offering less tracks but chucking in an additional exclusive, 'Lagoon', for good measure.

The song is flanked by two contributions from Sam Hardwick, reprising his role as the dead boy introduced on *Wishmaster*'s 'Dead Boy's Poem'. The spoken extracts feel intensely personal to Tuomas, imploring listeners to cling on to the innocence of our inner child, a wisdom coming from experience. From the off, we find the songwriter at a particularly low ebb and the atmosphere set for an affecting and raw record that would not only come to define Nightwish's sound, but also Tuomas's reputation as a sincere and open songwriter.

'End of All Hope' 3:54 (Music and lyrics: Tuomas Holopainen)
From the calm of 'Bless the Child', 'End of all Hope' unleashes a thunderous apocalypse. If Tuomas was resigned to his suffering before, he is now a zealous preacher, demanding his audience not to follow in his footsteps. The track wastes no time in introducing its refrain, which acts as a mantra throughout the song's four minutes, its unrelenting ferocity carried by the masterful drumming of Jukka Nevalainen. It soon becomes apparent why the song had the working title 'ReWishmastered', sharing a similarly vehement hook to 'Wishmaster' from the last full-length.

Without discrediting the necessity of 'Bless the Child', it feels like 'End of all Hope' is a second commencement with its blistering energy and a similar take on the album's theme; the song is unashamed to be the more forceful of the two and hammers home Tuomas' message to any metalheads that tuned out during the midtempo opener. 'End of all Hope's stance as an opening gambit was solidified when, alongside *Once*'s 'Dark Chest of Wonders', it was chosen to launch proceedings proper on the *Decades* tour in 2018 (if we discount the brief 'Swanheart' interlude from Troy Donockley of course).

The track gives way to a soaring guitar solo from Emppu in its middle eight, warming up any unimpressed power metal loyalists that may have been ready to switch off and the lyric gives a knowing glance to the band's early days, 'Angels they fell first, but I'm still here'; flipping the message of the *Angels Fall First* title track and, similarly to '10th Man Down' before it, envying those who had managed to escape the distress of life.

Century Child's first two cuts also share the honour of supporting videos, though 'End of all Hope' feels a little more cobbled together and wasn't given a physical single release. During the video, live shots of the band performing at 2002's Tuska Festival capture an energy that is nearly impossible to recreate in a stuffy warehouse or film studio. This time, instead of a tailored storyline, scenes from the Finnish movie *Kohtalon Kirja* (The Book of Fate) were incorporated. Marketed as a fantasy/horror movie, it lends much more of the latter including a creepy *Evil Dead*-looking thumbnail.

'Dead To the World' 4:21 (Music and lyrics: Tuomas Holopainen)
'Dead to the World' is the fans' first real taste of Marco Hietala as a vocalist, flitting between accompanying Tarja and taking the lead in the verses. Whilst the leading lady sounds as sensational as ever, it really is a moment of focus for the new bassist following nervous mumblings that having another vocalist on board may undercut the beloved Tarja and her contributions. As such, welcoming Marco into the fold with a song such as 'Dead to the World' was a wise move in appeasing the operatic-leaning fans and proving some assurance that the new line-up was an evolution rather than a complete overhaul.

As its title would suggest, the track isn't a particularly uplifting affair and discusses the harsh reality that it is one another that cause our suffering as opposed to the 'monsters under your bed'. The elusive, all-important hope remains through a rebirth ('innocence reborn once more') and what better time for a new start than a new century? 'Giving birth to the century child' is the only lyric that references the enigmatic album title, which may well have reflected the culture of a millennium renaissance during the early 2000s when the album was composed. As many pledged to give up vices, a return to his inner child was Tuomas' aspiration.

'Ever Dream' 4:44 (Music and lyrics: Tuomas Holopainen)

If 'Ever Dream' feels thematically disparate from the rest of the album, it could be its position as a brief respite from the permeating misery of the tracks surrounding it. Structurally and lyrically, it's the most instant track on the record and its ode to true love achieves the challenging task of remaining earnest without slipping into cloying and saccharine territory.

The song was lifted as the first single from *Century Child* and, despite not sharing too much of the album's encompassing theme, it was a strong choice thanks to its immediacy and a lasting legacy amongst fans. The single was backed with the anticipated Andrew Lloyd Webber cover 'The Phantom of the Opera' and a non-album track 'The Wayfarer', all three serving as a tasty starter ahead of the album's release a few weeks later. The single has since been certified platinum in Finland and managed to surpass gold status in two days.

As the song with which she auditioned for Nightwish, 'Ever Dream' became a crucial element of Anette Olzon's time with the band and remained in setlists during her tours with the group. Anette released her demo version of the track on social media site Myspace in 2011, demonstrating the warmth and charisma that landed her the enviable role as the new Nightwish singer back in 2007. 'Ever Dream' was less demanding of an operatic delivery, lending it perfectly to Anette's contrasting vocal style and offering itself for interpretation by the versatile Floor Jansen years later. Unsurprisingly, the song has appeared on setlists across every tour since its release, excluding only the *Decades* tour dates.

'Slaying The Dreamer' 4:31 (Music: Tuomas Holopainen, Emppu Vuorinen, lyrics: Tuomas Holopainen)

'Slaying the Dreamer' is quite the U-turn from the warmth of 'Ever Dream', marking the album's midway point with its heaviest moment. The misery that permeated the first few tracks is channelled into self-loathing anger, with Marco's raspy yells intertwining with Tarja's ascending trills.

Tensions in the band's relationship with Tarja surfaced publicly for the first time as Tuomas revealed that the composition was inspired when he was cornered by a friend of Tarja, berating him for mistreatment of the vocalist. Internalising the criticism, he told *Metal Rules*:

> I needed to soften some parts in my lyrics, because I cannot use too extreme phrases for the lyrics of Nightwish. There just needs to be a certain limit [in]

> how far I can go with my lyrical approach because our music is indeed far from being extreme, if you know what I mean. I did sow my hatred and gave vent to my temper enough on them already, I think.

Surprisingly for a self-berating song that must have been difficult to perform, 'Slaying the Dreamer' remained in the band's setlist until the *Imaginaerum* tour before being reprised in the *Decades* setlist. Though likely a challenging listen for Tuomas night after night, the heavy cynicism gave a dynamism to the live set and offered Marco the remit to demonstrate another side of his vocal capabilities, almost descending into a roar for the song's catastrophic conclusion.

'Forever Yours' 3:51 (Music and lyrics: Tuomas Holopainen)
There is a calm after the storm with the sparse and succinct 'Forever Yours'. Accompanied by the tin whistle of Kristiina Ilmonen, the song acts as a precursor to future ballads such as 'The Islander' and a continuation from the charming 'Swanheart'. Returning again to the embellishment of pipes and whistles, it set a foundation for Troy Donockley to join the band years later as a full-time multi-instrumentalist (with a keen steer towards uilleann pipes and tin whistles).

'Forever Yours' has a naïve charm as it recalls a life-shattering heartbreak. As the song bids farewell to a 'little broken heart', it evokes a hormonal teenager discovering their crush with another, but the song unpacks into a much more mature realisation. The crushing message ponders how the value and charm of life can be stolen away by grief to a point in which heaven itself has no appeal. Tying 'Forever Yours' to a late nineties classic which also dealt with romance and heartbreak, Tuomas commented to Perkele Magazine: 'If 'Bless the Child' is *Gladiator* style, then ['Forever Yours'] follows the line of *Titanic*.'

Charming as the song is, 'Forever Yours' feels a little by the book and suffers from the sequencing of *Century Child* as it, alongside the next two tracks, pale in comparison to the bookends of the record. The band seemingly agreed as they were also the only contributions not to be included in the World Tour of the Century live shows, nor in subsequent tours.

'Ocean Soul' 4:14 (Music and lyrics: Tuomas Holopainen)
It's remarkable that 'Ocean Soul' isn't a sprawling centrepiece of Nightwish lore, considering just how many times the phrase is mentioned across their discography. This title with which Tuomas adorned himself speaks of his adoration of the ocean, something he has documented ever since *Angels Fall First*. Not many people are so frank when it comes to their ideal way to die, but Holopainen strips away the grisly connotations as he details his death wish: to be swept away into the big blue. Despite its recurrence across the band's work, 'Ocean Soul' itself remains one of the more forgotten tracks in their discography.

Tuomas eventually confessed to barely remembering where the term came from, but 'Ocean Soul' is a recurring phrase mentioned across 'Dead Boy's Poem', 'Dead to the World', 'Bless the Child' and 'Lagoon'. It is also quoted as a centrefold in the album's booklet with the following text, signed off by the ocean soul himself and giving a concise summary of the entire album's theme:

> The only true love I ever knew was behind those downcast eyes. The only comfort I ever felt was during those long hours of loneliness when I felt for you. I do believe only innocence can save the world. Ocean Soul.

Musically, the mystical male choir underpins Tarja's despair in the opening verse but it's the tinkling synths that concoct the stinging frost of a wintery ocean breeze. There is a stark contrast in the organic chorus as these synths crash away, almost as if the song takes place in two very different mindsets, one of a sorrowful anguish and one of a clarifying resolve.

'Feel For You' 3:54 (Music and lyrics: Tuomas Holopainen)
Even at the time of promoting *Century Child*, Tuomas had little to say in regard to 'Feel for You', telling *Perkele* magazine: 'This song is hard to comment on, but it's still very powerful and expressive, at least for me. The arrangements were modified at least 66 times during the recording process'.

The track can be dissected into three parts, the first third characterised by a return of the chilly synths conversing with Emppu's guitars and Tarja singing of a tireless passion for a first true love. By the time the initial refrain appears at the halfway point, it's another moment for Marco's mighty presence to come to the fore, commanding the puppet girl of whom he is in total control. The closing minute is left to Tarja, who chants the mantralike second refrain, 'This one is for you, for you, only for you'; whether an enchanting devotion or a maniacal obsession – the mysterious 'Feel for You' remains open to interpretation.

'Phantom of the Opera' 4:09 (Music and lyrics: Andrew Lloyd Webber, Charles Hart, Richard Stilgoe, Mike Batt)
An instant standout when surveying the *Century Child* tracklist, it feels correct to see Nightwish tackle a song that is built on the foundations of drama, opera, and a heathy dose of darkness. The decision to cover the song came, as one may expect, from a viewing of the musical during one of Tuomas' visits to London. Naturally, its inclusion on *Century Child* was a point of questioning for many interviews at the time, including *Metal Brasil*, to whom Tuomas told:

> It was my idea, just like all the other covers we do. I love making covers! There are people who think it's ridiculous, say they don't do covers because

> they only value their own work. And in the case of this song, I always thought it sounded like a Nightwish song because of the melodies and even the plot, it looked like Nightwish! So we decided to do the cover our way…

Tarja herself was onboard with covering the popular track, an enviable opportunity to demonstrate the growth in her vocal capacity over the years. She spoke to *Metal Hammer* about the choice:

> Tuomas has been thinking that this song would fit Nightwish for a long time. I heard this song first when I was 12 or 13. Then I decided to become a singer. Today this musical is too smooth in my opinion. I prefer, for example, *Hair*. I really loved 'Phantom of the Opera', but unfortunately my performance isn't that brilliant. I wasn't able to get into a suitable mood. This siren-like singing doesn't fit me very good. There are lots of versions of this song, but I couldn't find my own access to the song. That's a pity, but we can't change it now.

Perhaps not on the recording but with a regular setlist spot across the following tours, Tarja went from strength to strength performing 'Phantom of the Opera', ably supported by a frenzied Marco taking on the role of the phantom and imploring the songstress to 'sing, my angel of music'! In a further brush with online virality following 'Ghost Love Score,' many YouTube reactors and reviewers applauded the *End of an Era* performance of the song, particularly noting the astounding power of Tarja's soaring vocal crescendo. 'Phantom of the Opera' was fairly retired from setlists during Anette's time with the group (Tuomas to *Metal Rules*: 'I don't think she will ever do 'Phantom of the Opera' because that was so focused on Tarja'), though a live rendition by Floor Jansen and Henk Poort on the Dutch TV show *Beste Zangers* had fans clamouring for its return to the Nightwish live set in future.

'Beauty of the Beast' (i. 'Long Lost Love', ii. 'One More Night to Live', iii. 'Christabel') 10:22 (Music: Tuomas Holopainen, Marco Hietala ('Long Lost Love'), Emppu Vuorinen ('One More Night to Live'), (lyrics: Tuomas Holopainen)
Now, this is what you call an epic! Combining the complexity of arrangements such as 'Lappi' and 'FantasMic' and the band's new appetite for an orchestral, cinematic scope, the enormous ambition we have come to expect from Nightwish could easily be drawn back to this very song. Comprised of three characterised but cohesive sections, 'Beauty of the Beast' rarely gets the plaudits enjoyed by tracks like 'The Poet and the Pendulum' or 'The Greatest Show on Earth'. One reason could be its inclusion on the band's last album before their biggest international breakthrough on *Once*, another could be its omission from setlists save for a handful of shows on the *Century Child* tour and a few Tarja solo renditions.

A masterpiece does not arrive easily, though and Tuomas expressed as much to *Atlantis*:

> The idea I had was to mix all the different elements of our music into the same song and try to make it as powerful as possible. We wanted to create a song that nobody could do bigger. So it had to be long, it had to have a ballad part, a bombastic part, and [Tarja's] vocals had to be in the focus. It ended up with the mixing guy having 140-150 tracks to keep an eye on. It was hard on them…

'Long Lost Love' mixes the best of *Century Child*'s slower side, a longing and understated introduction despite a rumbling orchestra looming menacingly in the background. It's also the first time Marco contributes to Nightwish's songwriting, with Emppu providing an input into the second section, rendering 'Beauty of the Beast' one of the band's most collaborative efforts to date. Emppu's presence is hard to miss on the pinnacle of the piece, 'One More Night to Live', which ups the tempo and the energy; it's the one segment of the epic that could likely stand alone on *Century Child*, though is undoubtedly amplified by its suitemates. Eventually, the album fades out just as it faded in and is once again adorned with the spoken word of Sam Hardwick. Musically, 'Christabel' is a beautiful final payoff of the sprawling track, but lyrically, we again hear reference of the dead boy as Tuomas marks himself a failure for the demise of his 'best play'. The title 'Christabel' is shared with an unfinished poem by Samuel Taylor Coleridge – the first part being completed in 1797 with additional components planned but never completed – 'a dead boy who failed to write an end to each of his poems'.

There is the album's persistent longing in the track, but another resolve appears to Tuomas: 'sanest choice in this insane world: beware the beast but enjoy the feast he offers'. We are implored to preserve our purity but also accept the inevitability of life's temptations. If the dispiriting laments on the album cast some worries for Tuomas' wellbeing, it is a brief consolation to hear him yearning for one more night, the glimmer of hope for the future. It's also a bittersweet realisation as he ponders, 'all of my songs can only be born of the greatest of pains', a beautiful silver lining during the beast of a lachrymose chapter.

'The Wayfarer' 3:24 (Music and lyrics: Tuomas Holopainen)
If you were pondering where the fun had gone on *Century Child*, you need look no further than its B-side 'The Wayfarer'. It's a powerful and lively jaunt from the off, with Emppu's wailing guitars carrying the listener throughout. The message of the song sits neatly next to *Wishmaster*'s 'Wanderlust' as it celebrates the journeys of life, forging forward to the next experience and discovery. A charming attribute of 'The Wayfarer' is the way it references two other *Century Child* tracks – 'One More Night to Live' from 'Beauty of the

Beast' and 'Dead to the World', tying itself firmly to the album it was ousted from. There's also as a link back to the Disney ode 'FantasMic' with the song's opening nod to Uncle Walt.

Tuomas revealed to *Perkele* magazine that the reason for 'The Wayfarer's exclusion was that it simply didn't fit on *Century Child*. Though the album's sequencing is crying out for an additional rush of energy in its second half, thematically, 'The Wayfarer' just feels too optimistic to make much sense and may well be better experienced outside the confines of the record as a tacked-on bonus track; it also offers an artificial 'happy ever after' to the bleak album theme.

The song was eventually released across numerous editions but was initially saved for the Japanese release of *Century Child*, as a B-side to 'Ever Dream' and as part of the *Bless the Child* EP. 'The Wayfarer' also came painfully close to being performed live on the *Imaginaerum* tour but was downvoted by Marco, who labelled it 'not a really good song'. Ouch.

'Lagoon' 3:46 (Music and lyrics: Tuomas Holopainen)

As demonstrated on 'Forever Yours', Tuomas showed a knack for lyrical restraint on *Century Child* – not always an easy ask when it feels safer to overexplain every bit of your intent. Similarly, on the bonus track, 'Lagoon', we have a sparsity to the words and message. Whilst some may recoil from its simplistic nature, it couldn't work better than with the tranquil verses and serene arrangement of this bonus track.

As with 'The Wayfarer', 'Lagoon' also offers a rare piece of optimism as Tarja philosophically discerns: 'feeling lonely and content at the same time, I believe, is a rare kind of happiness'. The refrain is primarily made up of layered vocalisations from Tarja with a soundscape much closer to 'Kiteen Pallo' and 'Sleepwalker' than the ten songs which made the album's final tracklist. Perhaps it was this very association that determined its fate as it eventually saw a release as the B-side to the 'Bless the Child' single though 'Lagoon' is also one of the few lonely B-sides to not make it onto Spinefarm's bolstered *Bless the Child* EP – probably to incentivise diehard fans to also purchase the single version.

'Don't Talk to Strangers' (Live Cover) (Music and lyrics: Ronnie James Dio)

With Marco on board and a new vocal presence to play with, a feast of heavy metal pioneers were now game for a live cover, as demonstrated on the *Century Child* tour. One track that received only a sole rendition was Dio's 'Don't Talk to Strangers', which a lucky audience in Germany were witness to. The song didn't feel a million miles away from their eventual Pink Floyd cover, 'High Hopes', which also relied heavily on Marco's impassioned and raw delivery.

The switch from tamer verses to a heavy chorus was an apt segue between the elegant 'Walking in the Air' that preceded it and the ferocious 'Slaying the

Dreamer' that followed in the setlist. There was a powerful weight to 'Don't Talk to Strangers', an emotional tangibility that could have been the reason for its omission in the dense emotion of the *Century Child* tracks; perhaps a more light-heartened respite was required in its place – Dio's loss was Ozzy's gain.

'Crazy Train' (Live Cover) (Music and lyrics: Bob Daisley, Ozzy Osbourne, Randy Rhoads)

Many songs tried, but few could compete with the sheer sticking power of 'Crazy Train'. It was melodic, invigorating and an antidote to what could have been an otherwise gloomy set. As *Century Child* shifted away from the power metal roots of the group's *Wishmaster* years, the cover of Ozzy Osbourne's solo debut was the ideal opportunity for Emppu to let loose. Marco excelled in the opportunity to take sole vocal responsibility, but it's the shredding guitar from Vuorinen that stands out – the energetic Finn racing his fingers through star solos and appeasing any attendees pining for the band's earlier material.

A memorable performance of the cover was filmed for the *End of Innocence* documentary DVD. It saw the band joined by tourmates Charon, keen to prank the headliners by dancing around the stage shirtless with upside-down crosses stuck to their chests. Nightwish weren't innocent in the capers, though, Marco sporting angel wings fashioned from paper and some fetching black briefs whilst dancing onstage for Charon's performance of 'Little Angel'. The other support act on the tour was none other than After Forever, featuring lead vocalist Floor Jansen, but it was guitarist Bas Maas that lent his talents to the band at their Tilburg show in 2002, guesting on the ever-popular 'Crazy Train' cover.

'We're Not Gonna Take It' (Live Cover) (Music and lyrics: Dee Snider)

Chant-along glam metal songs may not be the first thing that comes to mind when venturing into the *Century Child* era, but the cover of Twisted Sister's 'We're Not Gonna Take It' was another opportunity to sidestep the permeating gloom of the album's themes. Marco has rarely sounded more at home, slightly more guttural in his delivery than Dee Snider's original and a confident charisma that galvanised the crowd. The song was performed on a handful of German shows and one Russian venture, serving as an addition – rather than a replacement – to the regular cover 'Crazy Train'.

'Wild Child' (Live Cover) (Music and lyrics: Blackie Lawless, Chris Holmes)

From what is a relatively loyal cover of W.A.S.P's 'Wild Child', Tuomas' synth flourishes underline the anthemic chorus, somehow making it sound even more quintessentially eighties than the original. In the context of a Nightwish set, 'Wild Child' shoots for a similar tone as 'Crazy Train' but whilst the former feels more in keeping with the band's style (those keyboards lift it straight into *Wishmaster* territory), the impressive solo from Vuorinen just wasn't as impactful as on the Ozzy cover and Marco never sounded quite as alluring as Blackie Lawless managed on the original. Instead, it's Jukka's frantic crescendo and pounding presence that steals the show, battling with Tuomas' keyboards until the very last second with the drummer's usual boundless energy.

Once (2004)

Personnel:
Tarja Turunen: vocals
Tuomas Holopainen: keyboards,
Emppu Vuorinen: guitars
Marco Hietala: bass, vocals, acoustic guitar
Jukka Nevalainen: drums
John Two-Hawks: chanting, oration, flutes
London Session Orchestra: orchestra
Pip Williams: orchestra and choir arrangements
Sami Yli-Sirniö: sitar ('The Siren', 'Ghost Love Score')
Olli Halonen: slide guitar ('Creek Mary's Blood')
Jouni Hynynen: aaargghh (vocals)
Marc Brueland: spoken word ('Higher Than Hope')
Paul Clarvis: percussion ('Creek Mary's Blood')
Anthony Pleeth: cello ('Kuolema Tekee Taiteilijan')
Martin Loveday: cello ('The Siren')
Sonia Slany: violin ('The Siren')
Jenny O'Gady: choirmaster
Metro Voices: choir
James Shearman: orchestra and choir conductor
James Collins: orchestra engineer
Aaron Price: assistant engineer
Simon Goldfinch: second assistant engineer
GME Choir: GME noise
Gavyn Wright: orchestra leader
Recorded and engineered by Tero Kinnunen and Mikko Karmila at Tempputupa and Finnvox studios
Recorded between November 2003 and March 2004
Additional recordings at E-Major studios by Emppu Vuorinen
Mixed by Mikko Karmila with Tuomas Holopainen and Tero Kinnunen at Finnvox Studios in March 2004
Produced by Tuomas Holopainen and Tero Kinnunen
Mika Jussila: mastering
Toni Härkönen: band photography
Markus Mayer: cover art

Reaching the end of their contract with Spinefarm and Drakkar, Nightwish were scouted by record labels before signing with Germany's Nuclear Blast. The label had established themselves as a hotbed of leading metal talent and could offer an explosive amount of international exposure. Despite good relations with their former labels, it was clear that they had outgrown their more modest leanings; it was time for Nightwish to scale up again and dream big.

It doesn't get much bigger than a London session orchestra, either. Whilst the band had come to trust Tuomas' instinct when demoing new songs, even they were struggling to perceive the grand approach he was taking for the songs of *Once*. Not surprising either, since many of them relied heavily on an epic orchestral sound that just wasn't communicable via a keyboard demo.

For a band that would soon become just as well known for their symphonic sound as their riffs, Pip Williams became a prominent part of the Nightwish story. The orchestra arranger remarked that working on *Once* was one of the most enjoyable projects of his 35-year-long career and the arranger became a firm part of the Nightwish tapestry moving forward. Williams recalled his initial involvement with the band to *Kentapress*:

> In the late '90s, I had produced some tracks for Turkish rock band Mavi Sakal, which Mikko Karmila had engineered. For this, I had done some large orchestra arrangements. Mikko remembered this and recommended me to Tuomas and the band. This was in 2003. I get to understand his mind more with every project. At its most basic level, right from the *Once* album, we had meticulous briefing sessions and spoke a lot about his influences and what he wanted to get from me. His demos are very well prepared and he presents me with solid ideas for his orchestral parts. I believe we now have a unique relationship, where I have freedom to make my own contribution to the scores, while preserving his more definitive ideas.

Through this collaborative approach, Pip Williams was able to guide Tuomas into the expansive world of orchestration for which Tuomas was a keen student, telling Satu Reunanen at RockUnited:

> I went to London in the end of November with our demo and we went through the songs there. Then I showed him some parts with my keys, for instance, how I wanted the flute to go, where I want to have a trumpet and a harp. He worked on that basis for two months and then started the actual recordings. It brought a difference to the sound. Originally the idea was to have the orchestra only on a few songs or a few parts, but Pip Williams got excited about the whole thing so much, that he wrote each song over again from beginning to end. But I don't mind.

Press ahead of the album's release promised an album surpassing the grandeur of *Century Child* and all that had come before it. It achieved a record of the most expensive Finnish album ever made and hype only grew with the mention of the London Session Orchestra (unable to be marketed as the Philharmonic due to only 50 of the orchestra's 90 players being present on the recording). Tarja was particularly positive about the material, stating time and again that it was her favourite work and a record she had even been listening to in her own time. Feeling that the balance between her metal persona and classical leanings had been struck, Tarja reflected to *Metal Rules*:

> This is the first time for me personally when I can proudly say I'm one hundred percent satisfied with my vocal parts on this album specifically. Now I feel like my voice on *Once* is as natural and relaxed as it can be in the first place and I don't sound forced or artificial as I partly tend to sound on our previous albums. And this is actually what I have tried to achieve for Nightwish albums for so many years already.

Arriving to the world in Summer of 2004, *Once* was received with instant acclaim from critics, yet its legacy remains as the album that sparked a meteoric expansion of their fanbase, perhaps helped by a growing interest in female-fronted metal heralded by the commercial success of Evanescence. 'People tend to compare our music to Evanescence and it's very funny because there are not that many elements there that we have in common' Tarja stated diplomatically. All attention is good attention when it comes to promotion, however and with their most ambitious work to date at the helm, it surely didn't hurt if a few Evanescence fans happened upon them.

Fittingly, the singles from *Once* were the band's most infectious to date, providing a captivating taste of what the band had to offer for new listeners. 'Nemo' became a fan favourite upon its release as well as a setlist mainstay, 'Wish I Had an Angel' was another slice of immediate euphoria and, though not as obvious as the other singles, 'The Siren' proved that *Once* was not lacking when it came to diversity either.

Time has also been kind to *Once*. It birthed the viral hit 'Ghost Love Score' and was rewarded with multiple re-releases, most notably the stunningly packaged platinum reissue that tacked on the bonus tracks 'Live to Tell The Tale' and 'White Night Fantasy', and the remaster issued eighteen years later by Nuclear Blast. Tuomas commented on the latter:

> Nostalgia is a powerful tool. I easily remember what those days surrounding the release of the record were like. The excitement, the ambition, the comradeship, the triumphant tour to come, it was all there, about to carry the band to another level, musically and journey-wise.

With a new label and boundless aspirations, if there was a single album that turned the tides for Nightwish, it surely had to be *Once*.

'Dark Chest of Wonders' 4:34 (Music and lyrics: Tuomas Holopainen)
The perfect introduction to the cinematic bombast of *Once*, 'Dark Chest of Wonders' was a confident and triumphant taste of what the album had to offer. It might have been savvier to ease the listener in gently, but instead, 'Dark Chest of Wonders' parades its more-is-more approach with relish,

signifying a transformative era for the band in which the symphonic element that was dabbled with on *Century Child* would become a dominating force.

Once again, Tuomas concocted the majority of the album in private before talking through his ideas with the rest of the band. When it was time to discuss 'Dark Chest of Wonders', producer Tero Kinnunen just didn't understand what Tuomas was going for, saying the concept sounded 'messy', and drummer Jukka was just as perplexed. Once the pieces of the audio puzzle came together, however, all doubts were cast aside and Kinnunen shifted his suggestion of canning the track to making it the very first song of the opus.

The opening of *Once* also signifies a move away from the gloomy despair of its predecessor, venturing back to the world of fantasy, imagination and escapism with a gleeful refrain casting off the burdens of the past few years. By the time the track draws to a close, it's clear that the Nightwish of 2004 onwards would become a very different beast to the humble Finns of the Spinefarm years.

'Wish I Had an Angel' 4:11 (Music and lyrics: Tuomas Holopainen)

As a group of strangers began making moves on his girlfriend in a bar in Kitee, Tuomas was pissed off enough that a song idea sprung almost immediately into his mind. 'Wish I Had an Angel' drips with lustful desire as Marco selfishly longs for satisfaction in its chorus. The setting of the bar also seeps into the music as an industrial edge pulsates throughout as if Nightwish were recording next to a heaving nightclub.

It isn't the usual fare for the group, Tuomas himself calling it the most 'down-to-earth song' he'd ever composed; most fans likely expected the songwriter's inspiration to come from a serene lake or majestic cathedral rather than from propping up a bar, but the more humdrum muse is neatly disguised with Tuomas' flair for metaphor. Why sing 'sex' when the poetic 'virgin Mary undone' will do the job just as well? And what better way to symbolise betrayal than labelling the seductor as 'the thirteenth disciple'?

'Wish I Had an Angel' had one of the most immediate hooks in the band's history so it was no surprise to see it lifted as the group's second single from *Once*. Backed with a cover of the dance pop track 'Where Were You Last Night' by Ankie Bagger, the single became an unexpected disco venture for the Finns, a rare foray into hedonistic gratification undiluted by the esoteric matters that usually took precedence. A video for the single paled in comparison to the grand 'Nemo' promo but, like 'End of all Hope' before it, was padded out with clips from the 2005 horror flop *Alone in the Dark*. The movie's director, Uwe Boll, also acted as director for the 'Wish I Had an Angel' clip which was released in two versions, one of which omits the *Alone in the Dark* segments completely – perhaps a smart move following the film's accolades as 'worst picture', 'worst special effects' and 'worst director' at the Stinkers Bad Movie Awards.

'Nemo' 4:41 (Music and lyrics: Tuomas Holopainen)
A perfect single at the perfect time, 'Nemo' encompassed everything that *Once* had to offer in a neat, digestible four-and-a-half-minute package. The grand scope of the album needed an appetising figurehead and it's hard to think of a better candidate than 'Nemo' with its tinkling piano intro crashing into a heavy, melodic hook. It was unashamedly dramatic, all building to a tensive middle-eight and final, electrifying rendition of the chorus. Tarja's performance excelled, clearly taking note of her diction and providing clarity and restraint as well as the soaring power fans had come to expect. The response to the single catapulted Nightwish into the charts, reaching the top ten in Norway and Germany and hitting the top spot in Finland and Hungary. 'Nemo' was also the group's first appearance in the UK top 100; perhaps Tuomas and Pip Williams had been canvassing for listeners between the orchestra recording sessions?

The song is a staple in the Nightwish live set, another track that has been present across the eras of all three vocalists, and currently holds the record for the band's most performed song, surpassing over 600 outings as of August 2022. As proof of the legacy of *Once*, the only song within sniffing distance is 'Wish I Had an Angel', which has been performed over 500 times, album cuts 'Dark Chest of Wonders' and 'Ghost Love Score' also featuring in the top five.

A great song needed a captivating video and this was another place that 'Nemo' struck all the right chords. Directed by Antti Jokinen, the clip was undoubtedly focused around Tarja who appeared in a striking red coat set against the white snow and throbbing white lights. Discussing the song with *Metal Hammer's* Dom Lawson and Natasha Scharf, Tarja said:

> The video was dark but striking and colourful, and it was very gothic, we got a lot of gothic followers after that video! I don't think Nightwish ever considered themselves to be a gothic band, but we got a lot of appreciation. My friend is a Finnish tailor, and she's still in charge of many of my outfits. We had this idea for the red coat, a very strong colour against the snow falling. If you think of symphonic metal bands with female singers, they're usually dressed in black. I was always the weird girl with the weird voice, the operatic vocals, and then I wore this red coat! I still see girls at my shows dressed like me, so I guess it was really powerful. We had an initial 'No!' from MTV at the time, because they didn't want to show a video that was in the snow! We thought, 'Why are you showing beach videos all the year round, but you don't want to show snow falling?' Some TV stations were not willing to show the video, but it was a big thing for us. Many new people got to know us through that song.

In a trend of the time, one version of 'Nemo' was also interspersed with movie clips, this time from another poorly received horror movie, *The Cave*. One movie it had no affiliation with, however, was *Finding Nemo,* which just so happened to have been released at a similar time – instead, the track takes its name from the Latin word for 'nobody'.

'Planet Hell' 4:44 (Music and lyrics: Tuomas Holopainen)
To offset the relatively soft 'Nemo', 'Planet Hell' was included as a B-side to assure fans that the heavier side of Nightwish hadn't melted away in place of an orchestra. Whilst promoting *Once*, Tuomas considered it the 'weakest song on the album', a surprising admission for many listeners as the track soon became a firm fan favourite.

The song casts the orchestra in an entirely different role than the spirited charm of 'Dark Chest of Wonders', as on 'Planet Hell' it transforms into a threatening inferno devouring all in sight. Marco is a fierce narrator and Tarja his right-hand woman; the two are a menacing welcome committee along the river Styx in a savage takedown of human selfishness and injustice. Christianity and Greek mythology intertwine in the song; the 'first rock' referencing Jesus' claim that the first stone be cast by those without sin and Noah's extricating ark which Tarja asserts the world is not ready for. In the end, it's the ferryman Charon for whom we must all save a penny to grant our passage into the underworld, leaving behind a planet swept by damnation and suffering.

On a much lighter note, the song became an unlikely soundtrack to the Finnish gymnast Tiia Piili's winning aerobics routine at the FISAF World Championships in 2005. Her third consecutive win at the event, Piili's splits, spins and energetic bounding may not have been an obvious match for one of *Once*'s heaviest moments, but it's a galvanising soundtrack to a dynamic performance that celebrated the best of Finland in two very different fields.

'Creek Mary's Blood' 8:34 (Music and lyrics: Tuomas Holopainen)
Inspired by the book of the same name by American novelist and historian Dee Brown, 'Creek Mary's Blood' mourns the horrors of the 19th-century Native American genocide. The song doesn't hide behind allegories, instead serving as a powerful retelling from the perspective of a displaced native. The rousing first verse pays respect to the land and generations through which stories and traditions live on whilst the refrain mentions the trail of tears, the forced relocation of indigenous peoples, which included the Muscogee Creek nation to which the song title refers.

The central focus of the song is its guest contributor John Two-Hawks, a musician of Lakota, French, Anishinabe and Irish descent. The story of how he became involved with Nightwish was told candidly by Tuomas to *Me Naiset* in 2004:

> I have always had a fixation for the Indians, ever since I was a kid. The song that John appears on took heavy inspiration from Native American culture

> and his presence brought more dignity to it. I sent him a letter to Arkansas and I invited him to the studio. At first, he questioned whether we were a bunch of Satan worshippers, but it was soon resolved. John, in his dream, received an order from his forefathers to do this with us. His inclusion was a great honour for us.

The song swells into a magisterial peak that won't be matched until later epic 'Ghost Love Score', but 'Creek Mary's Blood' instead ends on a different note, offering its final minute and a half to the esteemed guest. The Lakotan poem is recited by Two-Hawks, expertly clenching the listener's attention as whistling pipes and forbidding percussion underscores. *Underground Empire* asked Tuomas about the language chosen:

> This is Lakota, a certain John Two-Hawks translated my poem from English. There just had to be a full-blooded Indian involved to give the song the finishing touches. I found him via Google, just typed in 'Native American Musicians' and found John Two-Hawks' homepage. I listened to his samples, flute playing and Lakota singing and thought he was perfect. I emailed him and had his reply the next day. I sent him a demo of the song to listen and rehearse, then we flew him in for five days, from Arkansas to Helsinki, just for that one song. But it was totally worth it! I don't think a single metal band has done anything like using an authentic performance instead of samples before. This song is also my personal favourite.

With a clear intent towards authenticity, it may have dismayed Tuomas when later online discussions pulled Two-Hawks' legitimacy into question. A young tribe member claimed that the Lakotan was actually gibberish and made little sense, while Two-Hawks countered back that the claims were slanderous. In press around the album's release, he told *Rock United* of the struggles of translation: 'English doesn't translate that well into Lakota. English is a language of words, Lakota is a language of concept'.

Despite his debated authenticity, it didn't prevent Two-Hawks from collaborating with Tuomas' future wife Johanna Kurkela on the Christmas release *Noel* and joining the group for their *End of an Era* show at Hartwall arena. The song has only been performed alongside Two-Hawks, with subsequent renditions in 2008 and 2009 on the *Dark Passion Play* tour.

'The Siren' 4:50 (Music: Tuomas Holopainen, Emppu Vuorinen, lyrics: Tuomas Holopainen)

On Islay, an island in the Inner Hebrides of Scotland, Fiona Middleton is known for serenading the seal population with her violin. The captivating tradition served as a starting point for the composition of 'The Siren', a considerably more harmonious muse than the cruel temptresses of Greek mythology. The merciless mythological sirens needn't feel affronted, however, as Tuomas spoke with Charlie Farrell from *Get Ready to Rock* about their impact on the final song:

> I just wanted to do something Eastern like Egyptian or Arabian. Then I saw the Disney movie *Sinbad*... there's this scene of about five minutes where the sirens come and tempt Sinbad and it has awesome music behind it, and I said, 'I wanna make a song about this' ... about Sirens tempting the listener – that's the whole idea of the song.

Structurally, the song is a unique creature with few lyrics and one repeated refrain rather than a hooky chorus. Tarja's whispered desires behind Marco's vocals are otherworldly, drawing on her alluring charm as she is cast in the role of the titular femme fatale. Marco leads us through his journey into seduction and a desperate confusion after succumbing to Tarja's lure before ethereal vocalisations are all that remain. Though she has significantly fewer lyrics, Tarja's dynamic performance is one of her best on the album, transforming to an unrecognisable calling at the song's midway point. In amongst all the surprises, a guest sitar slot from Kreator's Sami Yli-Sirniö punctuates the glistening charm of Tarja's chants, and the late Sonia Slany's electric violin gives an amplified nod to the Scottish siren that inspired the song.

Never afraid of an unconventional single choice, 'The Siren' was lifted as the fourth offering from *Once*. Big budgets also meant more promo and a third music video was commissioned; Nightwish were well and truly playing with the big leagues, but their egos were kept in check when the final result was revealed. An embarrassing animated clip, promptly wiped from the internet and still unavailable on YouTube, was universally lauded in the Nightwish camp. Its eventual limited release on the Nuclear Blast website lent credence to the adage of 'once on the internet, always on the internet' as it still lurks across smaller video platforms despite efforts to exile it from existence. A much more refined animation adorned the cover of the single, almost an EP in its own right, by including multiple versions of 'The Siren', a Megadeth cover and a live rendition of 'Kuolema Tekee Taiteilijan'.

'Dead Gardens' 4:33 (Music and lyrics: Tuomas Holopainen)

Tuomas was suffering from writer's block when it came time to compose *Once*, likely following the emotional purge of *Century Child* and the difficult topics that the album had unveiled. From his creative drought surfaced 'Dead Gardens', the first track for the album and a revitalising assurance for Tuomas that he still had plenty of songs inside waiting to be penned. He credits the song's inspiration as the Finnish group Kotiteollisuus for whom he has performed keys on numerous records, jokingly calling the song a 'total Kotiteollisuus rip off' to *Rock United*. Though he later commented that it's likely the weakest song on the album in hindsight,

Above: Nightwish with Tarja Turunen during the 2004 promotions for their last album together, *Once*.

Below: Now an international symphonic supergroup with former After Forever and Revamp vocalist Floor Jansen at the helm.

Left: Angels, they fell first, but they're still here. (*Spinefarm*)

Right: The debut single 'The Carpenter' was a split release with fellow Spinefarm acts Thy Serpent and Children of Bodom. (*Spinefarm*)

Left: From a 'swamp born' remake to a crucifix controversy, everyone had an opinion on the *Oceanborn* cover. (*Spinefarm*)

Right: Four ballads of the eclipse: three Nightwish ballads and one made-to-order classic for *Sleeping Sun*'s title track. (*Drakkar*)

Left: Deemed 'deeply unnecessary', the remake of 'Sleeping Sun' at least righted the wrongs of the song's promo video. (*Nuclear Blast*)

Right: What's in front of the boy on the *Wishmaster* cover? Tuomas: 'the very same text the owl is carrying on Oceanborn'. (*Spinefarm*)

Left: The band's first EP, *Over the Hills and Far Away*, foresaw the lengthy *Century Child* sessions ahead, offering 'something to the fans in the meantime'. (*Spinefarm*)

Right: Exit Sami Vänskä and enter Marco Hietala amidst a soundscape of orchestral majesty offsetting the mournful lyrics on *Century Child*. (*Spinefarm*)

Right: The right song at the right time, 'Nemo' soundtracked an unprecedented peak for the band's success. (*Nuclear Blast*)

Left: Ending on a momentous, if dramatic, high – *Once* was to be Tarja's swansong with the group. (*Nuclear Blast*)

Left: Bassist for Nightwish's power metal years, Sami Vänskä eventually grew bored of touring and was dismissed.

Right: The gothic overtones of *Century Child* seeped into the dark music video for album opener 'Bless The Child'.

Left: The smouldering songwriter and band leader; Nightwish may not be a dictatorship, but Tuomas Holopainen undoubtedly remains its figurehead.

Right: End of an Era: moments before firing Turunen, the band gave a momentous performance in Helsinki.

Left: Through turmoil and triumphs, Holopainen has steered the vehicle of spirit since 1996.

Right: Special guest John Two-Hawks joins the band in signalling the end of the triumphant *Once* era.

Left: *Dark Passion Play*: a welcome to Anette Olzon and a lifeline for Tuomas' mental health. (*Nuclear Blast*)

Right: Time for one more daring dream; the band's rebirth with Olzon was previewed on 'Eva'. (*Nuclear Blast*)

Left: 'Did we get this far just to feel your hate?' – 'Bye Bye Beautiful' pulled no punches. (*Nuclear Blast*)

Right: Are you ready for a little story? With tensions temporarily settled, imagination was the muse on the 'Storytime' music video.

Left: From Alyson Avenue to the metal masses; Anette Olzon embarked on her own eventful journey with Nightwish.

Right: 'A dream emporium' – *Imaginaerum* conquered new heights but at the cost of band relations. (*Nuclear Blast*)

Above: More than just a bassist, Marco Hietala delivered lead vocals on much of the band's post-2007 output.

Below: After seven albums behind the kit, Jukka Nevelainen left the band due to chronic insomnia in 2014.

Above: Please learn the setlist in 24 hours; flying Dutchwoman Floor Jansen helped Nightwish finish out the *Imaginaerum* world tour.

Below: Following contributions to *Dark Passion Play* and *Imaginaerum*, multi-instrumentalist Troy Donockley officially joined the band in 2013. (*Pat Pope*)

Above: Alongside Holopainen, guitarist Emppu Vuorinen is the group's longest-serving member.

Below: '…from so simple a beginning Endless Forms Most Beautiful and wonderful have been, and are being, evolved'.

Right: *Endless Forms Most Beautiful* tackled evolution, marvelling at the 'journey of us all' with biologist Richard Dawkins. (*Nuclear Blast*)

Left: A unanimous single choice (eventually), 'Élan' showcased more of Donockley than Jansen's versatile voice. (*Nuclear Blast*)

Left: Emerging amidst a global pandemic, *Human. :||: Nature.* dedicated an entire second disc to the natural world. (*Nuclear Blast*)

Right: Feast your eyes on the black mirror; 'Noise' criticised technology addiction with a striking promotional video.

Left: A headline set at Wacken 2013 catapulted the band to viral success, coining the term 'Floorgasm'.

Right: Kindred spirits Holopainen and Donockley would collaborate again on side-project Auri.

Left: Getting tribal; Wintersun's Kai Hahto stepped behind the drumkit following Jukka's exit.

Right: Fellow Wintersunner Jukka helped fill the Hietala-shaped hole at the band's virtual shows before being welcomed aboard officially.

Left: *Showtime, Storytime* immortalised a Wacken headline set and the hasty onboarding of Jansen. (*Nuclear Blast*)

Below: A virtual location for a virtual show, amidst the pandemic, the band reunited at the Islander Arms.

maybe the goodwill of its creative unshackling was what kept it on the record's eventual tracklist.

Admittedly, it's one of the few non-essential tracks on the opus, but it does beckon in a heavier mid-section of *Once*, the lyrics discussing the bare creative well from which it was scavenged. Some of the vocal lines feel unnatural as they're crammed in or elongated to fit the melody and, after the plentiful quality of the album's first half, the chorus of 'Dead Gardens' feels underwhelming at best. Without a doubt, the highlight of the song comes when it throws out the rulebook and descends into a cacophony that tosses out melodies in favour of a repetitive riff sounding like a stuck record, a perfect segue into the blistering 'Romanticide'.

'Romanticide' 5:03 (Music: Tuomas Holopainen, Marco Hietala, lyrics: Tuomas Holopainen)

Without even a second to recover from the chaos of 'Dead Gardens' ending, 'Romanticide' arrives just as vicious as its portmanteau title suggests. A compositional collaboration with Marco Hietala, this couldn't be more different from their other joint effort, the gentler closing track 'Higher Than Hope'. 'Romanticide' is riff-heavy and keen to demonstrate just how sinister an orchestral accomplishment can be when teamed with relentless guitar work. A gloriously purging beast, the track has made numerous appearances in setlists thanks to its riotous drama and incessant riffs, elements which would become less common in future albums in favour of a more symphonic, cinematic focus.

The song resolves to dismiss attempts at love unless something truly undeniable comes along – 'til love do me part'. It won't be an easy task as Marco sings of cold hearts turning to stone and harks back to an icy cold dead boy. Love letters burning, wine turning to water… it is rife with metaphor, religious allegories, and all to the same purpose of casting the frittering efforts of romance onto a raging pyre.

'Ghost Love Score' 10:07 (Music and lyrics: Tuomas Holopainen)

And here we have it, arguably the ultimate Nightwish song and, for many, an insurmountable peak in the band's career. It still remains a gateway for new listeners, it still remains an anticipated staple in their live set and it still continues to receive acclaim and commendations over a decade and a half later.

Though quietly confident of what he was about to unleash, surely the encompassing success of the song wasn't a presumption for Tuomas at the time, as he told *Rock United*:

> This is the biggest and the most ambitious song we've ever written. There's no sense in this either, the song has different parts and changes its atmospheres a lot. The song was originally called 'Ghost Love', but because

> of the nature of the song I wanted to include the score there too, so people will know what it's about. I worked this song to extremes.

Though 'sense' wasn't a priority for the lyrics, the resonating message of lost love permeates every second of the track, building to the passionate refrain which demands an audience chant-along. Naturally, it is a Tuomas composition after all, the song emerges from amongst the ocean waves, singing of sirens, the scent of the sea and blue memories before a bittersweet reminiscing on the idyllic recollections of what once was.

Following a plenitude of online reactions, Nightwish officially became one of the most reacted to acts on YouTube, rubbing shoulders with Korean record-breakers BTS and Japanese metal duo BABYMETAL. The commanding forces in the operation were threefold; the dedicated online community Nightdreamers Reacticide, the inevitable awe of 'Ghost Love Score' itself and lastly, the band's third vocalist Floor Jansen's transformative take on the song during the *Showtime, Storytime* performance at Wacken festival.

It will never be an easy job to tackle a song in which Tarja Turunen had carved such an inimitable, enchanting presence, but Floor Jansen went for reconstruction rather than direct recreation. Floor's malleable vocal skills twist from lyrical to operatic, from belting to almost spoken word across the ten minutes, but it was the grand finale that became the revered summit of her talents. A term was coined – 'Floorgasm' – for the innate response as the vocalist scaled ever-higher and more dynamic to match the orchestral swell of the song's closing crescendo, but how did it all come about? Fan Joel Flink asked Floor about the much-reacted-to moment: 'It just came naturally, actually. I just started singing it more free and Tuomas and the rest of the band liked it. Then after a few times, this ending 'appeared' as music is creative and unbound, and it was loved so much we kept it'.

Despite her clear vocal aptitude, Jansen was cautious in letting loose on a song that she describes as one of the hardest in the set to perform, telling Duke TV:

> [It's] one of the biggest challenges to sing, 'cause it's such a song to get it right. But I naturally felt that the ending … I always sang it differently, and it just kind of grew into the way it became ... I love playing the song always, because it became so special and because it comes out in a way that you can't predict.

Nightwish were tentative at first when it came to giving the song a live performance, though Tuomas assured fans that it would at least be attempted. With over four hundred live outings since, it's fair to say that the experiment was an overwhelming success. As the choir's chorus signals the intro and an inevitable rapturous reception, the beloved epic is unlikely to be leaving the setlist anytime soon.

'Kuolema Tekee Taiteilijan' 4:04 (Music and lyrics: Tuomas Holopainen)

For the first time since the group's debut, a song performed completely in Finnish was to be included on *Once*. 'Kuolema Tekee Taiteilijan' roughly translates to 'death makes an artist', Tuomas commenting to *Underground Empire* that it stemmed from 'the death of some of the things in my life that made me who I am now'. The title can also be read as a sobering recognition that many creators are only appreciated long after they have passed, surely not a thought far from Tuomas' mind as a songwriter fixated on his own oceanic demise.

It's the softest moment on the album, a respite from the epic drama of 'Ghost Love Score' and the darker, heavier songs that preceded it. This was a meditative moment of reflection and, whether a fluent Finnish speaker or not, the captivating emotion was undeniable through Tarja's powerful delivery and the mournful cello that punctuates the tragic beauty.

Describing the track to *Metal United*, Tuomas shared:

> I wasn't sure if should we include this on the album, but when Tarja sang her parts, we noticed that Finnish language works really well with this kind of a song, and it still didn't sound too pop-like. It's one of the best ballads we've ever done. The cello that was used in the solo cost three million pounds and it sure sounds like it too! But this song was basically written for the foreign people, that's why it's in Finnish. We always want to try new things, that's why we've got a Finnish song here, one with Lakota language and a techno song. And even though this song has only ten rows of lyrics, I wrote them the longest. It was really tough to get it right. This is about my personal feelings, but people can interpret them how they want to.

The song was another unexpected single choice, lifted as the third cut from *Once*, though this time without a music video. It had a limited release, focusing on the Japanese and domestic Finnish markets, reaching the top spot in their home country. The single comprised B-sides that were also present on 'Wish I Had an Angel' and later 'The Siren', including instrumental scores of 'Creek Mary's Blood' and 'Ghost Love Score' as well as a recording of the live Megadeth cover 'Symphony of Destruction'.

During her time auditioning for the band, Anette was requested to perform a selection of Nightwish classics, including 'Nemo' and 'Wish I Had an Angel', to help the band make their final decision. In an act of genius, the Swedish singer bravely took on the notoriously difficult Finnish language and covered 'Kuolema Tekee Taiteilijan' as a bonus inclusion on her demo. After joining the band, Anette chuckled, 'with my poor Finnish, they must have laughed their heads off'. It was Olzon who had the last laugh, however, as she reprised her Finnish to perform the song alongside the Sveriges Radios Symphony Orchestra at the Stockholms Kulturfestival in 2009.

'Higher Than Hope' 5:42 (Music: Marco Hietala, Tuomas Holopainen, lyrics: Tuomas Holopainen)

The tragic story of Nightwish fan-turned-friend Marc Brueland is told at length in the biography *Once Upon a Nightwish*, but his lasting impact remains as muse and posthumous contributor to this, the final song of *Once*. 'Higher Than Hope' tells the story of Marc's battle with a rare form of liver cancer, his passion for Nightwish and eventual meeting with them also told in his obituary at Invinciblestudios.com:

> While searching through compilation CDs for his DJ-ing sets, Marc stumbled across an album featuring a cover of 'Walking in the Air' by the platinum-selling Finnish heavy metal band, Nightwish. Through telephone conversations, Marc and the band's frontman Tuomas Holopainen became close friends. Marc travelled to Atlanta to see Nightwish perform at the Progpower concert and meet the band. During their performance, the band dedicated the song, 'Walking in the Air' to him and despite the near crippling effects of his illness, he was able to briefly walk out on stage. Marc and Tuomas shared a hug and Marc walked up to the microphone and said 'That's my brother', to the roaring approval of the crowd, many of whom had heard his story and were moved to tears. After developing a friendship and inspired by the strength and courage Marc demonstrated in his battle with cancer, Nightwish began to record the song 'Higher than Hope' for their album *Once* as a tribute to him. The song features excerpts of dialogue from a news interview Marc did after his first operation. Unfortunately, Marc passed away before he could ever hear his song.

The song is an uncensored account of Marc's suffering and, as such, it's far from a standard Nightwish ballad. 'Higher than Hope' is a powerful tribute, but it also delivers a harsh blow; cruel reality offset with the mounting courage that Marc displayed in his fight. In the end, it's the title refrain that sticks, the devastating realisation of a terminal diagnosis – an elusive cure is beyond even the most tenacious of hopes.

Though Tuomas was paramount in shaping the lyrics as an ode to Marc, the music was primarily led by Marco, who spread his intent wider than just his own bass and vocals as he told Reflections of Darkness:

> I play the acoustic guitar in the intro of the song and I wrote those lines. The melody lines of the vocals of the choirs and the verse are mine as well. I wrote a lot of stuff, not only the bass but the whole thing. I do write a lot of music when I am at home. I have a lot of things going on in my mind and I just put some things on a demo and gave it to Tuomas to check it over; see if something would have the Nightwish style. I immediately had the reaction when I wrote 'Higher than Hope' that this would be great stuff for Nightwish. The intro part has been with me for at least three years, but I had no song to fit it into.

'Higher Than Hope' brings *Once* to an emotional close, a cutting reminder of our own fragility, but also an echo of the band's own musical growth; from the campfire acoustics, mirrored in Marco's opening strums to the rhapsodic symphony that closes the track out, a braver and pioneering Nightwish defining themselves with astounding prestige.

'Where Were You Last Night' 3:52 (Music and lyrics: Tim Norell, Ola Håkansson, Alexander Bard)
For those metal purists who turned their nose at a 'Walking in the Air' cover, Nightwish putting their own spin on Ankie Bagger's 1989 pop hit 'Where Were You Last Night' will surely send shivers down the spine. The song was covered with a noble intent as Tuomas told Charlie Farrell from *Get Ready to Rock*: 'we wanted to make a statement 'Don't take us so seriously all the time, please''.

Still, there was no secret that this was about as B-sidey as a Nightwish B-side could get, Tuomas himself joking that the group would push to postpone its release as much as possible. Eventually, it saw the light of day on the 'Wish I Had an Angel' single, receiving a couple of Bon Jovi comparisons but all in all sneaking under the radar whilst the single itself caught the main glare of the spotlight.

With loud, proud synths, the track isn't a million miles away from Anette Olzon's post-Nightwish project The Dark Element and with its off-brand lyrical refrain, the song is a rare glimpse of the fun and irreverent side of Nightwish that had previously been confined to their wacky DVD documentaries. Whilst not likely to darken a setlist anytime soon, 'Where Were You Last Night' is an uplifting and successful stab at something very different indeed.

'White Night Fantasy' 4:09 (Music and lyrics: Tuomas Holopainen)
A logical continuation from the ethereal 'Lagoon', 'White Night Fantasy' conjures a similar atmosphere with its gentle, bewitching soundscape. As the clearest outlier from the *Once* era tracks, 'Where Were You Last Night' notwithstanding, it was a risky move to include it on the 'Nemo' single for fear it would give a wildly inaccurate idea of the album that was to come.

Though not nearly as kooky as the Icelandic visionary, Tuomas compared the song to Björk – more in the vein of her *Vespertine* release than *Once*, there remains an undeniable charm to 'White Night Fantasy'. Less about lyrics and more focused on ambience, Tarja whispers her way through the verses, beckoning you to lean in and pay close attention. It's a fascinating platform for her to demonstrate the softer, quieter side of her voice, her charisma remaining utterly riveting. No surprise then that it was Tarja herself who gave the song its long-awaited live debut during her solo shows, a surprising Nightwish rarity to rear its head amongst the more expected hits from her time with the group.

'Live to Tell the Tale' 5:04 (Music and lyrics: Tuomas Holopainen)
Ever critical of his own work, Tuomas wasn't shy about labelling 'Live to Tell The Tale' as 'the worst song I've ever written'. Still, most symphonic metallers would kill to have a track like this in their catalogue: warm synths, bombastic middle eight and a catchy chorus beefed up with some layered vocals on its final reprise. It's worth confessing that, had it been included on the final *Once* tracklisting, perceptions might not be quite as forgiving, but as a bonus track and B-side, 'Live to Tell The Tale' certainly deserves more love than its songwriter gives it. Thankfully Nuclear Blast wouldn't let Tuomas kill all his darlings and it was included in variations of the 'Nemo' single and tacked onto the platinum edition of *Once*.

'Symphony of Destruction' 4:19 (Dave Mustaine)
A live rendition of the Megadeth track 'Symphony of Destruction' was included on the 'Kuolema Tekee Taiteilijan' and 'The Siren' singles and though its title matched Nightwish to a tee, the song might not be the first one to spring to mind when it comes to obvious cover choices. Carefully navigating the trials of being an opera singer on the road with a metal group, a cover song with a solo vocal from Marco provided Tarja a mid-set rest and, should the situation require it, perhaps an outfit change too.

Marco is clearly at home on the metal anthem, giving an impassioned performance that truly takes flight in the chorus thanks to his maniacal rasps and commanding presence. 'Symphony of Destruction' feels much closer to his work with metal band Tarot than the duets he would often perform in Nightwish, but the group's familiar flair remains most evident in Tuomas' synth flourishes that underline the chorus and lift the reprised hooks, expertly reimagining what Megadeth may have sounded like if they had come up through the European metal scene.

'High Hopes' 7:20 (David Gilmour, Polly Samson)
Released somewhere between the *Once* and *Dark Passion Play* eras, 'High Hopes' was a newly recorded track on the *Highest Hopes: The Best of Nightwish* collection, also lending the compilation its title. Along with a remake of 'Sleeping Sun', its inclusion was likely to help lure in cash-savvy fans who weren't willing to splash out on a CD of material they already had – a smart bunch, that Nuclear Blast lot. The first few seconds of ambient noise may trick the listener into thinking 'High Hopes' is a studio cut until Marco's announcement and the roaring crowd appear – still, the high-quality recording was a welcome treat for loyalists as the lengthy wait for a new record sprawled before them.

The song was included as part of the Once Upon a Tour setlist, again to give Tarja a mid-set reprieve and offer Marco a few well-deserved minutes to soak up the spotlight. This time tackling the prog-masters Pink Floyd, less recreation was required, with Tuomas' frosty keys providing the perfect foundation. Marco switches from the characterful entertainer of 'Symphony of Destruction' to introspective crooner, dealing heavily in wrought emotion and a performance building from the first verse's nostalgic pondering to a commanding crescendo of its closing few minutes.

'Stone People' 4:09 (John Two-Hawks)
Whilst not a Nightwish song, 'Stone People' was included on the standout live release *End of an Era*. A John Two-Hawks solo taken from his 2004 album *Honor,* the track was a gripping and meditative interlude to 'Creek Mary's Blood'. The reflective vocalisations throughout 'Stone People' tease the soon-to-follow Nightwish epic, but the mesmerising performance captivates the audience in its own right – an elegant Two-Hawks floating through a smoke-covered stage, performing with a haunting native American double-flute.

Dark Passion Play (2007)

Personnel:
Anette Olzon: vocals
Jukka Nevalainen: drums
Marco Hietala: bass, vocals, acoustic guitars
Tuomas Holopainen: keys, piano, backing vocals
Emppu Vuorinen: guitars, acoustic guitars
Troy Donockley: bodhran, uilleann pipes, low whistle and tin whistle (on 'The Islander', 'Last of the Wilds', 'Meadows of Heaven')
London Philharmonic (credited as The Dark Passion Play orchestra): orchestra
Pip Williams: orchestra and choir arrangements
James Shearman: conductor
Haydn Bendall: orchestra engineer
Jenny O'Grady: choirmaster
Metro Voices and Metro Voices Gospel Choir: choirs
Guy Ellliott: lead boy soprano (on 'The Poet and the Pendulum')
Tom Williams: second boy soprano (on 'The Poet and the Pendulum')
Beverley Skeete: gospel solo (on 'Meadows of Heaven')
Tommy Blaize: gospel solo (on 'Meadows of Heaven')
Senni Eskelinen: electric kantele (on 'Last of the Wilds')
Nollaig Casey: Celtic fiddle (on 'Last of the Wilds')
Anthony Pleeth: cello
Martin Loveday: cello (on 'The Poet and the Pendulum')
Greg Knowles: cymbalom
Andy Findon: solo whistle (on 'For The Heart I Once Had')
Gavin Wright: solo violin (on 'The Islander')
Recorded between September 2006 and March 2007 at Finnvox, Abbey Road, Legendary E-Major and Petrax Studios
Arranged by Tuomas Holopainen, Jukka Nevalainen, Marco Hietala, Emppu Vuorinen and Tero Kinnunen
Mixed by Mikko Karmila at Finnvox Studios between April and May 2007
Engineered by Mikko Karmila, Tero Kinnunen and Emppu Vuorinen
Produced by Tuomas Holopainen and Tero Kinnunen
Co-produced by Tero Kinnunen and Mikko Karmila
Mika Jussila: mastering
Ville Akseli: band photography
Janne Pitkänen (ToxicAngel): album artwork
Gina Pitkänen: album artwork

Instead of riding high on the astounding success of *Once*, the era was drawn to a dramatic end as Tarja was dismissed from the band. Dating back to the composition of *Century Child* when Tarja declared it her final record with Nightwish, her relationship with the rest of the band remained turbulent and unpredictable.

Racked with guilt from not firing Sami Vänskä himself years before, Tuomas took this dismissal into his own hands and penned an open letter to the vocalist, co-signed by the other bandmembers. In essence, it stated that there was no future for Nightwish if Tarja was to remain a part of the group. Heated disagreements, a distant relationship following Tarja's hiring of her own manager and a US tour cancelled solely at the request of Tarja were just some of the factors given for the publicised firing. The open letter was shared with fans on the official Nightwish website and presented to Turunen immediately after the final show of the *Once* tour. The letter served another purpose, too, convincing the devoted fanbase of the risky decision. Parting ways with the face of the group and an operatic powerhouse that served as the band's trump card was a perilous move – and what a time to do it, at the very peak of their hard-earned success.

At a time when Tuomas would usually retreat to pull together new compositions, the focus was now on finding someone to sing them. Whether helped or hindered by their high profile, audition tapes flew in from across the globe and the Finnish press ran wild with speculations. In a full-circle moment, Theatre of Tragedy's vocalist Liv Kristine was heavily rumoured to be the successful candidate, having served as an inspiration for Tuomas years before. Metal Rules discussed the Finnish interest with Tuomas, who commented:

> Here in Finland … it totally got out of hand. Maybe we were a bit naïve and childish, but we thought this wouldn't be such a big hassle, but it truly was. In Finland, the Prime Minister even had something to say about the whole matter. It became like a national tragedy and a soap opera.

The band also poked fun at the rumours as they struck off a number of famous names (Liv Kristine, Sarah Brightman, Marcela Bovio from Stream of Passion and Tristania's ex-vocalist Vibeke Stene) before officially announcing Anette Olzon as their frontwoman in a website post. Hailing from Sweden and formerly the vocalist of AOR group Alyson Avenue, it was a refreshing surprise for audiences to see a new face behind the microphone rather than a familiar name that had been touted for months beforehand. Inevitably, many applicants will have been diehard Nightwish fans, but Olzon told *Tangra Mega Rock* that she wasn't hugely familiar with the Finns before auditioning:

> I hadn't listened to Nightwish that much. I had heard their name many times because I fancy the metal industry, but the first time I actually listened to them was just a couple of months before everything with Tarja happened. I think this is a good thing because now I can work with the band with clear eyes. I think the pressure upon me would have been bigger if I knew their whole history.

Wisely, Anette's identity was held back until just a few months before the release of *Dark Passion Play*. At the time of the announcement, Anette could be heard on the pre-release single 'Eva' as well as a number of snippets from the upcoming record. Still, anticipation was immense ahead of the September 2007 release of *Dark Passion Play* – not only was this the first record with Olzon, it was also the long-awaited attempt at following up the career-defining *Once*.

Anette's bright, pure vocal was worlds apart from Tarja – a conscious decision to deter the inevitable comparisons – and it fit perfectly with the vibrant lead single 'Amaranth', a masterful mix of the poppier side of Nightwish and a worthy platform for Anette's soaring voice. Curiously, almost the entire album was completed before Anette's hiring as vocalist, rendering her fitting performance on songs such as 'Amaranth' and 'Escapist' a work of pure serendipitous magic.

Elsewhere, the album was a vocally collaborative affair with Marco taking sole duties on 'Master Passion Greed' and the majority of 'The Islander', as well as playing an integral role in the mammoth '7 Days to the Wolves' and single 'Bye Beautiful'. It was also curious that the group chose *Dark Passion Play* to introduce a new tradition of attaching a full instrumental disc to the deluxe copies of subsequent album releases. An opportunity to explore the increasingly complex arrangements? Most certainly, but maybe also a way to appease any loyalists put out by the vastly different new vocalist.

The true heart of *Dark Passion Play*'s theme revealed itself in a later single 'Bye Bye Beautiful', which pulled no punches when addressing the Tarja tensions; it's this experience that permeates the entire album, from the frustration of 'Master Passion Greed' to the dejected 'The Poet and the Pendulum'. There is a nostalgic light at the end of the tunnel, however – whether it's the reflective, grand closer 'Meadows of Heaven', the ode to imagination of bonus track 'Escapist' or the folky respite in 'Last of the Wilds', there remains a beating heart in amongst the angst. In the end, Tuomas reflected on the album with poignancy to *Metal Hammer*: 'It would be an exaggeration to say *Dark Passion Play* saved my life, but it definitely saved my mental health'.

The turbulence of the previous years clearly didn't cease the ambition of the band nor put them off taking a few risks. The first is immediately evident: an almost fourteen-minute opener in the astounding 'The Poet and the Pendulum', a perfect scene-setter for the record both sonically and thematically, and elsewhere the album dips into AOR ('For the Heart I Once Had'), a return to acoustic-led balladry ('The Islander') and a gospel-metal finale ('Meadows of Heaven'). *Dark Passion Play*, just like its predecessor, was anything but predictable.

The odds may have been against Nightwish as they attempted to scale the heights of their previous album, but *Dark Passion Play* continued that confident upward trajectory, counting Iron Maiden's Steve Harris amongst its fans as he told *Metal Hammer UK*:

> When I heard *Dark Passion Play*, I couldn't believe it. I thought, 'Now, this is a proper fucking album.' It's got everything bar the kitchen sink in there. It was controversial because of the new singer, but she was brilliant. No disrespect to Tarja, but Anette's voice suited them a lot better. There's heavy stuff, classical, even a bit of Disney – all kinds of shit in there. I think it's one of the best-sounding albums I've ever heard in my life.

With approval coming from the mighty Maiden camp and a return to positive band relations, the rollercoaster of Nightwish's career was finally approaching another peak – not least in Finland, where *Dark Passion Play* eventually became the 31st best-selling album in Finnish history. The album also significantly raised the band's profile in the US, a difficult territory to break for European metallers, landing in the Billboard top 100 albums upon its release, peaking at number 84.

The Nightwish train seemed to be back on the track, and what does Tuomas Holopainen turn to when inner turmoil is off the table? Fantasy and imagination of course...

'The Poet and the Pendulum' ('White Lands of Empathica', 'Home', 'The Pacific', 'Dark Passion Play', 'Mother & Father') 13:53 (Music and lyrics: Tuomas Holopainen)

Immediately, *Dark Passion Play* confirms that it will not be sweeping the last few years under the carpet. Across a sprawling opening track, the scene is set with a fraught Tuomas firmly at its centre, no longer swathed in metaphor but mentioned directly by name. This is clearly his story.

'The Poet and the Pendulum' doesn't shy away from one particular inspiration, though admittedly, it would be impossible with a title so clearly nabbed from Edgar Allan Poe. *Sea of Tranquillity* quizzed Tuomas on the poet's impact:

> I'm a fantasy and horror freak. Poe is one of the best. *The Pit and the Pendulum* is one of my all-time favourite novels. I just loved the wordplay of 'The Poet and the Pendulum'. When I was writing that song, I was going through the most terrible time in my life because of what was going on with the band and elsewhere. Right now, it feels really awkward listening to that song, especially playing that song, since I'm not that person anymore. But I just fancied the idea of killing myself in a song, in a concrete way. In the lyrics, it even says in the lyrics that 'Tuomas was buried...' Now it feels really weird to listen to that song, but at that time, it felt like the ultimate catharsis that I had to do. I imagined myself being on an altar with the pendulum coming down like in the novel and that's where the song was born.

Whilst Poe's short story has a last-minute escape from the maws of certain death, 'The Poet and the Pendulum' slaughters its own composer, a warming rebirth emerging in the final utterance of the song as it announces 'the beginning'. It truly is a purge of the foreboding years that informed its composition, the demo version later included on the 'Bye Bye Beautiful' single, including a number of cut lyrics. If the eventual inclusion of the fretful chorister agonising of being 'raped again and again' felt troubling, the original lyrics were even more disturbing: 'Would you like to rape my rotting carcass? Dissect my heart and dislocate my wrist. It would make you come, wouldn't it?' This initial depravity was rejected outright by the choirmaster, resulting in a comparatively tamer final edit.

The track also takes a steer from the acclaimed 'Ghost Love Score' which created an appetite for an ascending zenith on every Nightwish album thereafter, though this time also leaning into 'Beauty of the Beast's multi-part structure, each section appointed its own title and narrative scope. 'White Lands of Empathica' takes its title from a location in Stephen King's *The Dark Tower*, lending its opening stanza to the aforementioned young male soprano. Soon after, a driving refrain first appears in 'Home' and later reprises in the desperate mid-section peak of 'Dark Passion Play', the panicked chaos of the descendent pendulum eventually evaporating before the introspective 'Mother and Father' provides the all-important hope to battle on.

Just one track into *Dark Passion Play* and devoted fans were already appeased; the group were more than able to reach the dizzying ambition of *Once*, some listeners even arguing that the distraught poetry of 'The Poet and the Pendulum' surpassed 'Ghost Love Score'. The epic became yet another setlist peak and, as further proof of its prominence on the record, it was very nearly lifted to be the title of the record. Next, it was time to settle some scores with Tarja ...

'Bye Bye Beautiful' 4:16 (Music and lyrics: Tuomas Holopainen)
The metaphors are thinly veiled on 'Bye Bye Beautiful', the clear and cutting response to former vocalist Tarja and the tensions that saw her ousted from the group. It's the more poetic, indirect verses that are graciously assigned to Anette Olzon, the only member of the group to not be involved in the drama that inspired the song. Save, however, for Marco's interrogative chorus, 'did you ever read what I wrote you? did you ever listen to what we played?', an accusation that Tarja had betrayed the unassuming sentiment behind Nightwish's music. Wisely, in the strident middle-eight, Tuomas acknowledges that eventually, the pain will subside – at that moment, though, the searing pain of the 'red-hot blade' of Tarja's words were impossible to ignore.

The song was lifted as the fourth single from *Dark Passion Play*, a likely choice thanks to its electronic undertones that mirror the roaring success of 'Wish I Had an Angel'. Though a dance remix of any Nightwish song will come as a surprise, this felt the most fitting for DJ Orkidea to contort into the winding twelve-minute club anthem that rounds out the single release.

The most memorable aspect of the single promotions was the tongue-in-cheek video in which the group are steadily replaced by female models. Tuomas commented that it had no relation to Tarja's firing and was, in fact, a response to accusations that they had hired Anette for her appearance, in order to appeal to more fans. It succeeds in giving a light-hearted touch to the deeply personal song and was supported with a DVD release that incorporated the promotional clips for 'Amaranth', 'While Your Lips Are Still Red' and 'Bye Bye Beautiful' as well as a making-of featurette for the latter.

'Bye Bye Beautiful' quickly became a fundamental part in the Nightwish story, but the reason it was created later became the very reason it was resigned to the vaults. Once the flames of the band's fury had started to diminish, so did the urge to parade their dirty laundry onstage, even if it had fast become one of their most well-known singles to date.

'Amaranth' 3:53 (Music and lyrics: Tuomas Holopainen)
It's remarkable that Anette's first real moment as leading lady doesn't arrive until almost twenty minutes into *Dark Passion Play*. Yes, she is fundamental to the striking opening track, but the sheer awe of its ambition exceeds the sum of its parts and her merciful backseat on 'Bye Bye Beautiful' was a necessary evil. The wait is worthwhile – 'Amaranth' simply cannot be contested as the perfect introduction to Olzon's vocal capabilities. The track drips with the shimmering magic of the keys and the cheerful bursts of the orchestra, yet it's Anette that is rightfully central, commanding the song with her charismatic delivery.

Musically, it is a clear choice as lead single from *Dark Passion Play*, even if it gives nothing away about the despair of its parent album. Fans living under a rock may have even expected a buoyant, joyous record if 'Amaranth' was anything to go by, but a little dig into the lyrics showed the realistic Holopainen emerging – the song isn't just a benevolent ode to optimism, but a recognition of the courage and daring that is often required to persist through the challenges. Perhaps because of this departure from the lyrical content of most of *Dark Passion Play*, 'Amaranth' was close to being relegated to a B-side as Tuomas told *Brave Words*:

> It's so corny and poppy and annoyingly catchy. I was laughing when I was writing it, thinking, 'Oh man, this is going to be something.' The funny thing about the song is that it was going to be the bonus track until the very end. I didn't like the song that much so it was going to be the B-side for the second single, but everybody kept telling me that it was awesome, that it was single material and the catchiest song on the album. I was laughing at myself when I wrote it because I knew it was going to work, I knew it was going to be good and that everyone would like it, but the chorus is just so pop-music.

As predicted, yet more success beckoned with 'Amaranth's release; a number one single in Hungary, Spain and Finland, the latter of which providing yet another gold certification in only two days to recognise sales of over 5,000 copies. As well as the fan favourite 'While Your Lips Are Still Red' and an orchestral version of the pre-release track 'Eva', the single previewed how *Dark Passion Play* was shaping up before Anette's contributions by including a demo of 'Amaranth'. 'Reach', the original title of the song, demonstrated how vastly the songs were transformed in the rehearsal and recording space, an unrecognisable chorus standing out as a section that was rightly given a necessary revamp before Anette laid down her vocals. 'Reach' is not a patch on the eventual recording but was a fascinating insight for curious fans, as its inclusion had intended.

Initially threatening a rehash of the questionable clip for 'The Carpenter' with a similar expansive mountain-scape, the music video soon delves into a much more cinematic focus. As the band perform in a subterranean lair chock-a-block with wind machines, the music video pays tribute to the painting by fellow Finn Hugo Simberg titled *The Wounded Angel*. As two boys rescue the bleeding angel, the townsfolk are filled with suspicion, casting her into a burning house from which she bursts into light, ascending once again. An appropriate analogy for the album that 'Amaranth' was the precursor to.

'Cadence of Her Last Breath' 4:15 (Music and lyrics: Tuomas Holopainen)

The tables turn on 'Cadence of Her Last Breath' as we find Tuomas observing somebody else consumed with the self-flagellation he usually reserves only for himself. Though Marco's backing vocals implore him to 'run away', Tuomas is enraptured with the woman, the 'breath-taking butterfly' that is centred in the song. Whether he is bewildered by his own urges to guide the lost soul or feels too powerless to help is open to interpretation, Tuomas admitting on Nightwish.com that during the recording, nobody seemed to really comprehend the message of the song:

> A very personal song though others don't seem to understand what it is about. There's running away in this track. Then having a crush, falling in love and then running away again… Other band members like 'Cadence of Her Last Breath' more. Personally, I think it's OK but not one of my favourites.

The chugging guitars underline Tuomas' concerns that the song would feel 'too much like American metal', though the usual symphonic dosage helps shift them away from any US counterparts. The demo version of the song released on the *Made in Hong Kong (and in Various Other Places)* compilation makes his worries a little clearer with tinnier drums, straightforward riffs and Marco's vocals proving a more palatable sound for a mainstream metal crowd. The one thing the demo does, unfortunately, drop is an ominous apocalyptic effect just before the song descends into its head-banging middle eight.

'Cadence of Her Last Breath' is a perfect breather after the storming opening trio. By no means a bad track, it's less impactful than the majority of *Dark Passion Play* and with early discussions pegging it as a lead single, it's clear that the final cut just wasn't up to par with the likes of 'Amaranth' or 'Bye Bye Beautiful'. The track had its moment in the sun during the *Dark Passion Play* tour but has not graced a setlist since. Still, Marco remains a fierce defender of the song, choosing it as one of his top 10 favourite Nightwish songs when talking to *Louder Sound*:

> I have a soft spot for 'Cadence of Her Last Breath'. In some ways, we didn't get as far with it as we wanted to when we recorded the song in the studio – we wanted it to be a little bit more impressive. I think it's got a lot of potential, especially when we play it live, and it's different to a lot of other Nightwish songs; the rhythmic structure and how the melodies go over it is unique.

'Master Passion Greed' 5:58 (Music and lyrics: Tuomas Holopainen)
Anette is once again given a backseat for 'Master Passion Greed', another song delving into the Tarja situation, though this time with an even sharper tongue directed towards her husband and manager, Marcelo Cabuli. Initially, Olzon had been tasked with half the lyrics, but it was Marco that suggested he perform it in its entirety, considering the sensitive subject matter. He discussed the song with *Pop Matters* and contrasted it to 'Bye Bye Beautiful':

> With 'Bye Bye Beautiful', it's a way of saying goodbye. In a way, that song is not actually lyrically as aggressive as it sounds … the whole lyric, I think, is more regretful; it's sad.' As for 'Master Passion Greed', I guess [it] really comes out of this sense of just hitting your head to a wall every time you try to arrange something, to work out something.

'Master Passion Greed' needed a ferocious soundscape to convey its message and the grand, hellish orchestra and aghast choirs evoke a sinister atmosphere for Cabuli's trial-by-song. Jukka is the irrepressible foundation as his drumming energises the savage verses, opening up to a vast and intimidating chant of the title lyric. Elsewhere insults are slung, though naturally with more of an artistic flair than a usual squabble: 'Judas', 'Leech in a mask of virtue' and a seemingly endless thesaurus of greed synonyms make clear that the venom had not completely dissipated since Tarja's dismissal.

The song has never been performed live, one of only two of the album's tracks that have the dubious honour, and things are unlikely to change in the future as Marco reflected to *SubMerge* magazine about the inspiration for the song: 'It's just something I'd rather forget about'.

'Eva' 4:26 (Music and lyrics: Tuomas Holopainen)
With the announcement of Anette Olzon as vocalist, the focus turned to how her voice would fit with the Nightwish sound. In between desperate clambering for copies of her work with Alyson Avenue and a short snippet released by the band, many fans couldn't resist the temptation of a leaked copy of 'Eva', the first Nightwish song with Olzon's vocals, that was doing the rounds online. Scheduled for release on May 30, to coincide with the reveal of Olzon's identity, the song was eventually rushed out on the 25th in response to the rapidly spreading leak.

It was clear that 'Eva' was chosen with the sole responsibility of introducing Anette's voice to the Nightwish audience. The ballad is firmly within the Nightwish wheelhouse, and the lyrics once again tell of a tragic loss of innocence, this time the story of a mistreated young girl. Fans expecting a long-awaited, all-guns-blazing Nightwish comeback had misunderstood the intentions of the release, a promotional taster but certainly not a formal lead single by any measure.

Capitalising on the interest in their search for a new vocalist, the group aligned with the message of the song to donate their European income from 'Eva' to children's charities in Germany and Finland. In 2007, a total of €10,000 was donated to the German foundation Die Arche, consisting of proceeds from the single.

'Sahara' 5:46 (Music and lyrics: Tuomas Holopainen)
It's not a surprise that in the midst of the troubles, a healthy dose of escapism was required – 'Sahara' is a symphonic gem that is often overlooked in favour of *Dark Passion Play*'s more ambitious compositions. Tuomas has made no secret of the fact that the story of 'Sahara' was, quite literally, dreamt up, telling Darkside.ru:

> This song is totally based on the dream I had. It's not like there is a real life behind this song, no. It's the dream that I had one night about this guy who is fleeing in Sahara like 5000 years ago. It's a kind of fantasy.

Less about the story itself, 'Sahara' is focused on transporting the listener to ancient Egypt. It goes without saying that this trip is a little more adept than 'Tutankhamen' on *Angels Fall First* with every aspect of the layered sound considered. Anette's vocalisations that close out the track cast her as a formidable desert siren whilst the male choir chant as the labourers constructing the pyramids. The rumbling orchestral percussion drops in and out like collapsing sand dunes whilst the strings soundtrack an Arabic venture through the titular desert.

'Whoever Brings the Night' 4:16 (Music: Emppu Vuorinen, lyrics: Tuomas Holopainen)

After the orchestra-dominated 'Sahara', 'Whoever Brings the Night' pulls the focus back to the core band; no huge surprise then that the music was left to guitarist Emppu Vuorinen. Worlds apart from his previous power-metal-oriented contributions, the guitarist still grants himself a long-awaited guitar solo in the middle eight. It's one of the only real surprises that 'Whoever Brings the Night' has to offer, a trundling mid-tempo with guitars that sound impatient to be unleashed.

If 'Sahara' was a retake on 'Tutankhamen', this song re-treads the tricky eroticism of 'Nymphomaniac Fantasia', again looking to the weak restraint of the seduced but thankfully without the cringe-inducing lyrics. It bears none of the romance of previous dabbles with love and lust, emphasising an almost depraved desperation between the two one-night lovers. 'Whoever Brings the Night' also demonstrates a maturity in the songwriter's style, Tuomas now able to cast a lustful ambience without crudely spelling out each detail. Vanessa de Campos asked him whether the song had been inspired by groupies, to which he clarified:

> Not about groupies, no. It's a song about the real dirty side of the human mind. Sometimes you get really scared about the wrong thoughts and dreams. But this is more like the sexual side and the really dark side of the human mind. That's what the song is about.

'For the Heart I Once Had' 3:56 (Music and lyrics: Tuomas Holopainen)

Even in the press release discussing the songs of *Dark Passion Play*, Tuomas was not exactly raving about 'For the Heart I Once Had'. At best, aligning it with the melody of 'Nemo' and, at worst, reducing it to just a necessary tempo-switch, he summarised:

> 'For The Heart I Once Had' was almost left out, but in the end, we kept it. At some point, it seemed that we were doing either very heavy or very soft songs for this album. Without this track, even though it's not the best one, there wouldn't be anything in between. I can't be blamed for similar tempos – every composer has their manners. To my mind, I avoided the worst clichés and tried uncommonly different things.

In an album of maximalism, the track was always going to have a difficult time. The song leans closely into AOR territory, much more suited to Anette's band Alyson Avenue than anything Nightwish had put their name to before. From the opening duet of guitar and piano, the song has a light touch that again steers away from orchestral dominance. It stands out for the vocal performance of Anette, effortlessly tackling the soaring chorus and its satisfying key change.

'For The Heart I Once Had', along with 'Master Passion Greed', remain the only two *Dark Passion Play* songs that have not been performed live – both for very different reasons. Whilst the latter was rife with passion, this track simply didn't get much love from the group themselves, Jukka allegedly not caring much for it, according to Tuomas in the group's Nightmail feature.

'The Islander' 5:06 (Music: Marco Hietala, lyrics: Tuomas Holopainen)
If earlier songs were righting the wrongs of *Angels Fall First*, 'The Islander' confidently journeys back to the band's initial acoustic objective. Almost solely performed by Marco with Anette offering some harmonising backing vocals, it was restrained in a very different way to the two tracks that came tracks before it.

Troy Donockley, at the time a session contributor, delivered a remarkable performance on uilleann pipes and whistles, transporting the song to a gusty seashore long before the music video had been dreamt up. Echoes of the muse from 'The Siren' emerge as Gavin Wright's violin ripples around the pipes and drifts wistfully into the horizon.

Quiet moments during a metal band's set are few and far between, but the challenge for a Nightwish ballad is particularly tricky, going head-to-head with 'Sleeping Sun' or 'Walking in the Air' to name but a few. Still, 'The Islander' commanded its spot and remained a staple in future tours, including a guest-spot duet from Sonata Arctica's Tony Kakko at Rock in Rio. It also meant that Nightwish no longer needed a Marco-led cover song to give the lead vocalist a break, 'The Islander' slipped into proceedings perfectly as Anette was granted a couple of minutes respite before joining for the second half. It garnered praise from the ever-critical mastermind himself, too, as Tuomas named it as a highlight of the band's set, a necessary reprieve from the encompassing bombast of the group's usual material.

The music for 'The Islander' was composed by Marco, an unsurprising contributor considering his heavy presence on the track, the bassist telling *Tuonela* magazine:

> I wrote the music for the song, and then again, it's something totally different from the rest of the live set. You have very few elements there; the main thing is the acoustic guitar and then the vocal line, and all the rest is basically just the background. You've got to create the tension and captivate people with the acoustic and with the vocal line. And those are the essentials that you've got to make it work.

During promotions for his solo album *Pyre of the Black Heart*, Marco remarked that Tuomas' appreciation of the song was a confident boost for his own songwriting, particularly those compositions with a Celtic steer.

Another boost likely came when 'The Islander' was released as the fourth single from *Dark Passion Play*, as the band were afforded yet another promotional video from Nuclear Blast. Whilst a simplistic seaside-at-dusk video would have been fitting, the clip's director Stobe Harju had grander ambitions. The band sit inside a circle of fire, offsetting the dim surrounding landscape as the story takes place around them. An undeniable steampunk influence, complete with obligatory flying ships, suspends above the titular islander; as he eventually lays down his anchor, fans are treated to a sneaky easter egg – a cameo from future member Troy Donockley. If 'The Islander' video cemented any relationship, however, it was between Tuomas and director Stobe Harju who would later go on to direct the feature-length film and album companion *Imaginaerum*.

'Last of the Wilds' / 'Erämaan Viimeinen' 5:41, 5:11 (Music and lyrics: Tuomas Holopainen)

It was perhaps the most surprising single of the band's career when the instrumental track 'Last of the Wilds' was lifted as the second promotional cut from *Dark Passion Play*. Wisely, the group were not quite plucky enough to bank on an instrumental alone and recorded additional vocals for the single release, retitled as the Finnish translation 'Erämaan Viimeinen'. The single was given a limited release in Finland and as a covermount in Germany's *Metal Hammer* magazine.

The translated lyrics tell of a wistful being, all thundering loneliness and traversing dreams, as he succumbs to his own eventual return to the earth below. As he surveys his own grave, the last part of the wilderness that he will encounter and become one with, there's a bittersweet tenderness to the song that makes it hard to place the tone – a celebration or commiseration? Musically, at least, the party is rousing.

Non-native speaker Anette Olzon was gracefully invited to step away from the Finnish lyrics, instead welcoming Jonsu Salomaa from the band Indica. The choice was both personal and practical – Jonsu offered a pure, child-like quality to her delivery that wasn't a million miles away from Olzon herself, thus remaining cohesive to the 'reborn' Nightwish sound. Tuomas was also a fan of Indica and took a drunken punt on inviting Jonsu to guest, as the singer recalled to *Radio Metal*:

> …he was a little bit drunk, maybe he was disappointed the next morning! It was after one of our shows at the famous Tavastia rock club in Helsinki. He told me he'd been a big fan of Indica since the beginning, and he asked if I could do one of their songs. I appreciated him as a composer already then, so of course, I agreed.

Indica would later support Nightwish on multiple tours, though unfortunately, never taking the opportunity to recreate 'Erämaan Viimeinen' live. The collaborations continued, however, with Tuomas producing the band's fourth album *Valoissa* and its English-language follow-up and Nuclear Blast debut, *A Way Away*.

With no discredit to Jonsu's winning performance, it's the instrumental that reigned supreme as a setlist regular on the first half of the *Dark Passion Play* tour and for the duration of the *Imaginaerum* dates. 'Last of the Wilds' took a confident step towards the folkier influence that has remained present on all subsequent Nightwish records and cemented the involvement of guest musician Troy Donockley. As a band that required a faultless finesse in their usual material, it was an opportunity to let loose and hail the spontaneity that it was created with, as Tuomas told *Rock Hard Valhalla*:

> To tell the truth, I don't even remember if this song was born like an instrumental track. We just let it roll to see what would happen with it in London, in the additional records. Then we heard the performance of Troy Donockley and Nollaig Casey with their Irish instruments. They were there, jamming this song so delightfully… It is like a cool war between Ireland and Finland, you know? We have Emppu on the guitars and Senni Eskelinen playing the kantele, a typical Finnish instrument, and they have their Irish instruments… Everything works on this music, I love the final result. It really makes you want to be drunk and start to dance around.

'7 Days to the Wolves' 7:03 (Music: Tuomas Holopainen, Marco Hietala, lyrics: Tuomas Holopainen)

Usual business is restored with the pounding drum intro of '7 Days to the Wolves', a threatening piece that brings to sonic existence the inexorable cruelty of time. Before each rendition of the storming chorus and its titular mantra, a brief silence is left; a pause to reflect or perhaps an oblivious look-up in panic. Likely edged forth by the struggles that birthed 'The Poet and the Pendulum', Tuomas again implores his audience to seize the moment, commenting on *Nightwish.com*:

> I'd say this song has the best chorus in the album. And you can really feel Walt Whitman in the lyrics. 'Leave the city of fools' or 'The road less travelled by'... Later on Whitman became one of my favourite poets, next to Edgar Allan Poe. I read *Leaves of Grass* quite a few times. The lyrics have a clear message: we only have one life, so we have to make the most of it. Carpe diem! The wolves are breathing behind you all the time.

A quote from Walt Whitman was included in the artwork for *Dark Passion Play* and the writer would indeed become a prominent influence on the band's follow-up record. Shortly after the *Dark Passion Play* tour wrapped, Tuomas would heed his own advice and bury himself in his beloved world of imagination and the awe-inspiring reverence that had temporarily been put aside to address the difficulty of the previous few years. The wolves had howled and Tuomas was keen to heed their warning.

Despite a commanding chorus, '7 Days to the Wolves' is unafraid to push the song structure in unexpected directions. As Anette delivers the impending line 'this is where heroes and cowards part ways', the song breaks with the expected formulas to descend into a pummelling gallop, a charming violin solo and a forceful raspy delivery from the frontwoman embodying every bit of urgency that the song required. From one final reprise of Marco's chorus, dripping with caution and immediacy, the hurrying race reaches its final stretch – but is the crowd running towards their own holy grail or merely rushing in panic towards their demise?

'Meadows of Heaven' 7:10 (Music and lyrics: Tuomas Holopainen)
Through the wrought emotional landscapes of *Dark Passion Play*, it's only fair that a semblance of a happy ending awaits – for Tuomas, that warmth could only exist from the nostalgic innocence of youth, the beating heart of the closing track 'Meadows of Heaven'. Long before the trials and tribulations of Tarja's dismissal and subsequent challenges, Tuomas' longing for purity had been omnipresent in his songwriting, searching tirelessly for it in others and berating the loss of it in himself. In the end, it's by looking back that he is able to return to the comfort of youth, a realisation that whilst he may no longer be able to attain his innocence, there's a radiating beauty in reminiscing on the clarity of childhood.

As the song progresses through its seven minutes, the hefty orchestra threatens to envelop the entire arrangement, yet 'Meadows of Heaven' reaches out its inviting arms – at once welcoming and daunting in its grandeur. Olzon sings of rocking chairs without dreamers and swings without laughter, conceding the role of deferential humans and daring to dream of a harmonious existence no matter how trite that may sound. After the tumultuous emotions of *Dark Passion Play*, it's difficult to begrudge an unbridled dream or two.

After the entire record has shifted through the cheer of 'Amaranth' to the angst of 'Master Passion Greed' and back to the celebratory 'Last of the Wilds', 'Meadows of Heaven' needed an extra kick to lift it to a higher plain. Tuomas was also keen to deliver yet another surprise to an audience who may have thought that the group had thrown out everything in their arsenal already. Speaking to *Rock Hard Valhalla*, Tuomas explained the idea and eventual impact of the gospel elements in the song's finale:

> I intend to always raise new things, try and experiment with new elements in our songs. After *Once*, I started to think: what kind of music could exist in the world and we didn't try to do yet? … Suddenly, I realised that the gospel choirs are amazing, because it has a very strong sound, people sing in a very genuine way. Then I said we would need to have one of these choirs in the new album. I told Pip Williams about the necessity of a gospel choir in a song and he booked one of these, which made a

> wonderful job in 'Meadows of Heaven'... and that part with the solos [at the end of the song] was totally improvised! Those people never heard the song before starting recording it, actually. They just started to sing those 'Heaven, heaven' in every possible way. I told them they could do whatever they wanted, except to mention the words 'Jesus' and 'halleluiah', then they started to laugh, and that made me realise that they have a good sense of humour.

'Meadows of Heaven' was given its live debut at the closing show of the *Dark Passion Play* tour at Hartwall Arena in Helsinki. Just as it had crowned the completion of the album, it also marked the end of a hugely successful string of almost 200 live dates around the world. In what many may have considered an unfeasible task, surpassing the numerous peaks of their most ambitious and challenging album to date, Nightwish had achieved the impossible once more. 'Dreambound for life', the songwriter penned ahead of the middle eight; on Nightwish's next album, he would make good on his promise.

'Escapist' 4:58 (Music and lyrics: Tuomas Holopainen)
Whilst online discussions of topics such as the best vocalist or best Nightwish album are always rife and heated, Nightwish fans are seemingly united on one front in particular – the unfair relegation of 'Escapist' to B-side status. The joyous, symphonic romp is one of the catchiest, finely crafted tunes from the whole era and, just like 'Dead Boy's Poem' and 'Ocean Soul' before it, was a concise testimony of Tuomas' evolving persona.

Its omission from *Dark Passion Play* didn't completely expel its fanbase, British magazine *Kerrang* choosing it as one of the top twenty greatest Nightwish songs in a 2021 retrospective, whilst 'Escapist' achieved what many bonus tracks could only dream of by being included in the setlist for a number of tour dates in 2009. It has also been afforded multiple releases– inclusion on the Japanese edition of *Dark Passion Play*, the B-side of 'Bye Bye Beautiful', an additional track on the German *Metal Hammer* issue of 'Erämaan Viimeinen' and the DVD edition of 'The Islander', the opening track on compilation *The Sound of Nightwish Reborn* and on live release/ compilation *Made in Hong Kong (and in Various Other Places)*. A bonus track it may be, but 'Escapist' is far from a rarity.

The song's legacy was cemented when Holopainen, on the brink of announcing an upcoming solo venture, repurposed a fan site named The Escapist as his official homepage. It's easy to see why, too; the lyrics offer a bittersweet insight into the battle between freedom and the necessary bounds of reality with another reference to King's *The Dark Tower* and plenty of nods to earlier Nightwish work; the first verse references the dead boy and the recurring image of the owl that was prominent on *Oceanborn* whilst the chorus reframes the songwriter's unending quest for innocence.

'While Your Lips Are Still Red' 4:25 (Music and lyrics: Tuomas Holopainen)

If nothing else, *Dark Passion Play* offered the most tenacious bonus tracks in the band's history. Just as 'Escapist' bolted out of the shadows, 'While Your Lips Are Still Red' began its ascension as the group's most triumphant B-side. Performed in over a hundred setlists to date, including an immortalising slot on the Wembley 2015 setlist recorded for live release *Vehicle of Spirit*, the song was initially dreamt up when director and neighbour Markku Pölönen came knocking. He asked Tuomas if he'd be interested in penning a track as the theme for his upcoming film, *Lieksa!* (The Matriarch), a Finnish drama to be released in 2007.

In promotion of the movie, the song was also given a music video, likely going some way in expanding the song's listenership above and beyond most other B-sides. It was also released ahead of the album itself when anticipation was reaching fever pitch, desperate fans clambering for a taste of how the post-Tarja Nightwish was shaping up. The video was a relatively simple affair, it featured a smouldering Marco and a stalkerish Tuomas trailing behind whilst clips from *Lieksa!* were interspersed. It hung together much more cohesively than the shoehorned horror clips of albums past. Despite plenty of video experience, it still didn't come naturally for Tuomas – especially as he was sans keyboards for the clip, he told Radio Metal:

> When you have the music, when you have your instrument, you feel like yourself. This is what you can do. But when the director says 'Action', and you have to do some things like… I had to throw this thing against the wall and look really miserable or hug this little girl and take her on my lap and play the piano with her. And I was just like: 'What the hell do I have to do next? Hold on… Oh yeah, now I have to look miserable!' It was really hard.

Written by Marco and Tuomas, 'While Your Lips Are Still Red' sings of an optimistic presence and youthful romance, expanding from a sparse vocal-piano duet to an impassioned peak topped off with a stirring violin solo. With only Jukka, Tuomas and Marco from the band performing on the song, the press release for the video described it as 'not exactly a Nightwish track', but that hasn't prevented it from becoming a firm fan favourite since its release. Initially emerging as a B-side to 'Amaranth', it saw subsequent inclusions on the *Made in Hong Kong (and in Various Other Places)* and *The Sound of Nightwish Reborn* compilations as well as the addition of its music video to the DVD release of 'Bye Bye Beautiful'.

'The Heart Asks Pleasure First' 4:20 (Music: Michael Nyman, lyrics: Tuomas Holopainen)

Despite their mastery of revamping soundtrack classics such as 'Walking in the Air' and 'Phantom of the Opera', Nightwish struggled to get approval from composer Michael Nyman to cover 'The Heart Asks Pleasure First', the rousing theme from the academy-award-winning film *The Piano*. Perhaps put off by Tuomas' decision to write lyrics to the previously instrumental piece, plans for the song to be released during the *Dark Passion Play* era were thwarted. From a faint glimpse of hope, however, the song did see the light of day. The Nightwish version of 'The Heart Asks Pleasure First' premiered at the very last second when it was played as the outro tape for the final show of the *Dark Passion Play* tour at the Hartwall Arena in Helsinki. It would spend the next few months traversing contracts, publishers, and approvers before it was given the go-ahead for a release during the succeeding *Imaginaerum* era.

Notwithstanding the newly composed lyrics, bursting with Holopainen's signature imagery, it's the timeless melodies of Nyman's original piano arrangement that remain the song's most striking feature. The Nightwish cut beefs up the soundscape with mournful strings and a wailing guitar solo, as well as just enough orchestra to go toe-to-toe with its *Dark Passion Play* peers. Yet it's when the song returns Tuomas' piano to the fore, reprising the original's enchanting melody, that the piece weaves its enchanting spell once more.

'Hilma Ja Onni' 5:04 (Music and lyrics: Jaakko Teppo)

Featuring on the 2009 tribute compilation *Pörsänmäen Sanomat – Tribuutti Jaakko Tepolle*, the Jaakko Teppo cover 'Hilma Ja Onni' is easily one of Nightwish's deepest cuts. Spearheaded by multi-hyphenate Jari Hyttinen, the collection reinterprets seventeen songs from Finnish folk singer Teppo's career. With Marco at his raspy best on vocals and a suitably heavier sound than the original, a sinister edge is given to this story of a woman leaving her partner and their farm for another man. Vowing to crash her wedding and fart in protest, the hectic comedy draws to a sombre note of reflection as the lonely protagonist sits alone.

'Finlandia' (Live Cover) (Music: Sibelius)

Ever the proud ambassadors for their country, 'Finlandia' – as its title suggests – is rooted in nationalistic history. Written by renowned composer Jean Sibelius, the tone poem served as a thinly veiled protest against the restrictions of the Finnish press under the censorship of the Russian empire. In the Nightwish sphere, it served as a Troy-led intro on the *Dark Passion Play* tour before being reprised as a mid-set interlude during the *Imaginaerum* dates. Troy's evocative pipes lift the patriotic anthem firmly into familiar territory, the Brit paying homage to the presiding Finnish presence in the band; 'Finlandia' confirms that, despite a newly inducted Swede on vocals, Nightwish remain proud of their status as beloved Finnish exports.

Imaginaerum (2011)

Personnel:
Anette Olzon: vocals
Jukka Nevalainen: drums, percussion
Marco Hietala: bass, vocals
Tuomas Holopainen: keys, piano
Emppu Vuorinen: guitars
Troy Donockley: bodhran, Cumbrian chanting, uilleann pipes, low whistle and tin whistle
London Philharmonic (credited as the Looking Glass Orchestra): orchestra
Pip Williams: orchestra and choir arrangements
James Shearman: conductor
Thomas Bowes: orchestra leader
Steve Price: orchestra engineer
Mat Bartram: orchestra engineer assistant
Metro Voices and Young Musicians London: choirs
Jenny O'Grady: choirmaster (Metro Voices choir), choral coordinator (Young Musicians London Choir)
Lynda Richardson: choirmaster (Young Musicians London choir)
Kai Hahto: additional percussion
Pekka Kuusisto: solo violin
Paul Clarvis: ethnic percussion
Stephen Henderson: ethnic percussion
Jussi Tegelman: soundscapes, music box
Guy Barker: solo trumpet
Dirk Campbell: sorna
Dermot Crehan: hardanger fiddle
Recorded between October 2010 and April 2011 by Mikko Karmila and Tero Kinnunen.
Recorded at Finnvox Studios, Petrax Studios, Marco's Cockpit, Röskö Campsite, Angel Studios, Pajarin Hauta and Legendary Bay of Tube Studios
Bass and guitar recorded by Emppu Vuorinen and Marco Hietala
Arranged by Tuomas Holopainen, Jukka Nevalainen, Marco Hietala and Emppu Vuorinen
Mixed by Mikko Karmila at Finnvox Studios between April and June 2011
Engineered by Mikko Karmila, Tero Kinnunen and Emppu Vuorinen
Produced by Tuomas Holopainen
Mika Jussila: mastering
Ville Akseli Juurikkala: band photography
Janne Pitkänen (ToxicAngel): album artwork
Gina Pitkänen: album artwork

There must be something about Walts. After Disney acted as influence in the band's earlier years, it was Walt Whitman that served as a muse for the band's

next venture. By this time, Tuomas' scope had inverted, turning away from the awe of religion and lore, and focusing in on a more humanist approach across *Imaginaerum*, something which would become even more evident on subsequent releases. Taking its title from Whitman's poem, 'Song of Myself' serves as the multi-part crescendo of the record whilst 'The Crow, The Owl and the Dove' gives nods to another writer, Henry David Thoreau. At first, it may have seemed that Holopainen had tightened his gaze, yet what could be more boundless and expansive than the human experience?

Speaking to *Metal and Macabre*, Tuomas gushed of his adoration of Whitman and the eventual composition of 'Song of Myself':

> I've tried to tell people about Whitman, I've given *Leaves of Grass* as a present and I've gotten really mixed responses. Some people really get it and some don't get it all. He really nailed the essence of existence, life, love and beauty like no one ever before. It was like it was written for me personally, and I wish people all over the world would share the feeling that I had. I've always enjoyed life, I've never been that depressed 'life sucks and were all going to die' guy, it's just that the world has never been better and more beautiful to me than it is now... I wanted to do something similar without it being a rip-off, but the point is I just wanted to observe the world my way as Whitman clearly did in his poem, just write down the thoughts as I see the world: certain situations, occasions, happenings here and there and just try to nail it and see what comes out.

As its title suggests, *Imaginaerum* was an affectionate ode to the human imagination. It was the bridge between Tuomas' fascination with innocence and his reverence of the natural world, never more present than on the aforementioned 'Song of Myself', which draws a strong link between the two. Elsewhere it explores the self-imposed horrors we subject ourselves to ('Scaretale'), the macabre beauty of a dying wish ('Rest Calm') and the limitless universes that exist in our own imaginations ('Storytime').

Never ones to shy away from upping the ante, the entire record was to serve as a companion to a full-length fantasy movie of the same name, directed by 'The Islander' collaborator Stobe Harju. Initially titled *Imaginarium*, an agreement was made to switch the spelling 'in order to avoid mix-ups with various things named Imaginarium' – potentially also to distance itself from the unrelated Hollywood movie *The Imaginarium of Doctor Parnassus* released three years earlier.

It may not have reached the dizzying heights of *Pink Floyd – The Wall* or *Purple Rain*, but the film was a charming visual aid to the album. It also featured short cameos from the members, which secured it as a must-watch for loyal fans, though perhaps not quite as essential viewing for casual listeners or the wider public. Never shy about his love of scores and soundtracks, if nothing else *Imaginaerum* was a fulfilling passion project for

Tuomas and resulted in the release of a primarily instrumental score a year after the main album's release.

Director Stobe Harju looked back on the film with a typical Finnish honesty when speaking to The Podcast and the Pendulum:

> At times it was very painful, not because of the band or the story or the movie-making itself but because of the all-surrounding politics. At the point where it wasn't really the band's movie anymore, I fought my fiercest battles, there was so many of them, but if it wasn't for Markus Selin (producer), Tuomas and myself, you'd have seen a completely different kind of movie. The last six months of the production and after seeing a version in the screening, I got the re-cut rights back and me and my incredible editor friend Mathieu Bélanger made the most of the time we had to make that recut.

Making drama on the big screen may not have proven viable, but drama in the ranks was something all too familiar for Nightwish. Despite a few bumps in the road, the *Dark Passion Play* tour presented a band that was once again united as they tackled an impressive two hundred shows worldwide between 2007 and 2009. Almost halving the number of shows, the *Imaginaerum* tour should have been less strenuous. Fast forward to halfway through the expedition and the night of 28 September in Denver, Colorado, when the Nightwish story took yet another unexpected turn.

A hospitalised Anette Olzon was unable to perform, leaving the band to scramble together a setlist with support act Kamelot's vocalists Alissa White-Gluz (also of Arch Enemy) and Elize Ryd (Amaranthe). Whilst the group sighed in relief that the show was able to go on, the signs of unrest with Olzon began to appear as she posted to her personal blog:

> I was never asked if it was OK they used Elize and Alissa in the show [Friday] night. I don't think it's a good decision they made and I'm sorry for those of you who came to see the whole band but got something else. But I was very ill and this decision wasn't mine. This is just music. Like life, sometimes we get ill and shows do get cancelled. Rihanna wouldn't ask Britney Spears to sing for her if she was ill. To think a show is more important than the humans in the band is, for me, so totally not in this world.

Still, one more show with Olzon was to go ahead the following night in Salt Lake City with 'Last Ride of the Day' an appropriate final performance as a group. Yet another scramble began as Nightwish and Anette Olzon officially parted ways following two records together, though the group remained resolute that no further tour dates would be cancelled. Incredibly, they pulled it off by inviting 'flying Dutchwoman' Floor Jansen to join the group in time for their next scheduled show in Seattle on 1 October 2012.

Jansen was known to many for her work with After Forever, a band that had also toured as support act to Nightwish years earlier. Prior to their disbandment, the Dutch group were also leading names in the symphonic scene and counted Epica's mastermind Mark Jansen as a founding member. Still, despite Jansen's glowing credentials, it was yet another moment of relief as the band exited the stage in Seattle. Somehow they had managed it, against all odds. Clearly astonished by their own achievement, the erratic backstage saga was filmed in the cheekily titled 'Please Learn the Setlist In 48 Hours' documentary.

As the turbulent era drew to a close, the *Imaginaerum* tour had one final surprise in store. A headlining set at Germany's Wacken festival was to be filmed for a live release, a memento for fans to tide them over between *Imaginaerum* and its successor. The riotous reception of *Showtime, Storytime* was astounding for the group as they had their first real taste of viral success. As of April 2022, Floor's metamorphic take on 'Ghost Love Score' had amassed over 1400 reactions on YouTube, solidifying Nightwish as one of the most reacted to bands in the world.

The reward for this unexpected union came in Autumn of 2013 when Nightwish announced that Floor Jansen was to become their permanent lead vocalist. Long-time session and live contributor Troy Donockley was also welcomed into the fold on pipes, expanding the band to an international six-piece and hinting at a folkier future. Once more, all eyes were on the group, wondering if the beaten and bruised Nightwish could thrive following yet another frosty line-up change.

'Taikatalvi' 2:35 (Music and lyrics: Tuomas Holopainen)

A music box ticks through its stark melody and winter descends. Before the stories begin, the two-and-a-half-minute intro 'Taikatalvi' paints the scene – white waters, moonbeams and lost summers – it is true to its title, roughly translating as 'Magical Winter'. Marco lulls through the gentle build, with an unsettling err to his delivery. *Imaginaerum* is an album about boundless imagination and dreams, it seems to warn, but where there are dreams, nightmares are also lurking. The duality was exhibited during the song's handful of live outings; revealed in silhouette behind a pale curtain, Marco serenades from a rocking chair before violently tossing it offstage.

'Taikatalvi' is an unusual opener for Nightwish, who have generally steered clear of the challenging Finnish language and had never before felt the need to kick off an album with an intro. It's worlds away from the enormity of the fourteen-minute launch of their last record, but it's unjust to write off 'Taikatalvi' as merely an expendable interlude. As with many Nightwish songs that came before it, the song honours the chilly Finnish landscapes, but this time they are to serve as a backdrop to the human experience. As Tuomas commented on the band's website: 'this world is but a canvas for our imagination'.

'Storytime' 5:23 (Music and lyrics: Tuomas Holopainen)
As Floor Jansen has taken to introducing the song live: who's ready for a little story? The first song proper and lead single from *Imaginaerum*, 'Storytime', is overflowing with the album's theme. Bursting from the cosy home of 'Taikatalvi', it's an enthusiastic venture that feels no guilt in retreating back to childhood. The song is a return to the early years of Nightwish too, Tuomas drawing again on treasured Raymond Briggs favourite *The Snowman*; 'How would it feel to take a midnight flight with a snowman through the most wondrous landscapes, like in the classic animated Yuletide film?' Tuomas asked on the Nightwish website. Rather than a recreation of *Oceanborn*'s 'Walking in The Air' cover, 'Storytime' instead invokes the adrenaline of soaring across a peaceful winterscape. If the Howard Blake original was a tranquil eyewitness to the magic, 'Storytime' propels us alongside the airborne pair.

Ironically, the song isn't a story as much as a celebration of existing tales. Peter Pan is name-checked, as is his home in neverland, but the song is much more concerned with the pure act of weaving a tale. It looks on in awe as a writer imagines whole worlds, tasting the impossible and pondering the intoxication of falling deep into a story. The words feel like a rebirth for Tuomas, unshackled by the cathartic writing of *Dark Passion Play* and rediscovering the freedom of his role as composer and imagineer.

In a satisfying turn of the tables, when the 'Storytime' music video was released, it was the band's own film that was interspersed with their performance rather than the horror-flops of eras before. The band shots lean into the storybook theme with Anette's *Snow White* garb and a nod to the theatre with Tuomas' *Phantom of the Opera*-style mask. Clearly, the visual creativity was reserved for the *Imaginaerum* movie rather than the 'Storytime' music video, though the juxtaposition of the humble behind-the-scenes shots and the confident band performance served to demonstrate just how charismatic the group had become following years of touring.

As the internet reigned supreme, tempting bonus tracks and B-sides for varying territories were less of a concern; after all, the songs would soon end up online anyway. This, paired with the financial burden of the movie, may have contributed to the lack of diverse content on the 'Storytime' single, which featured only a single edit, album version and instrumental of the title song. It certainly didn't impede on any success, however, with 'Storytime' returning the band to the top spot in Finland and reaching the top two in Spain and Hungary's charts.

'Ghost River' 5:23 (Music and lyrics: Tuomas Holopainen)
The flight of the snowman reaches a chilling descent as the ghost river snakes into view. It isn't as family-friendly as the festive story, but *Imaginaerum* is keen to gather all the nuances of life, as Tuomas commented when the album was released: 'life is the ultimate privilege; a river filled with wonders and

horrors. Love, sorrow, beauty, evil and temptation. And we need them all to survive and enjoy the journey. Good, Evil, Pain and Pleasure'.

'Ghost River' is the temptress that unleashes a darkness that comes to take hold in later songs, a gateway drug into the enticing appeal of wickedness. The haunting chants of the Young Musicians London choir cast Marco as a sadistic Pied Piper, luring children into the darkness and reminding us of our adolescent years, so often punctuated by a disturbing keenness to shed our own innocence – 'It's a scary ride we'd give anything to take'.

In keeping with the storytime theme, Marco's role as the aggressor references *Snow White* and bridge-dwelling trolls, whilst Anette adopts a maternal tone, insisting to 'never lose your heart' as she begs us to come across; Tuomas described the two characters to Metal Italia as 'the devil and mother Gaia'. As the river before us crashes its tumultuous waters, we're given the choice to cross and reach a utopian haven. The risk? The threatening river itself that has taken the lives of the choral ghosts. As the song spirals into its grand finale, 'Ghost River' ends as it began with a winding Van Halen-inspired guitar riff – the two bookends mirroring the adjacent riverbeds, perhaps we made it across after all?

'Slow, Love, Slow' 5:50 (Music and lyrics: Tuomas Holopainen)
Could it be a hallucination from the exhaustion of wading through the ghost river or are we now in some smoky jazz club with... is that Nightwish as the house band?! Both *Once* and *Dark Passion Play* proved that Tuomas just couldn't resist tossing in a few surprises and 'Slow, Love, Slow' is the first real jaw-dropper of the record. Primarily the song shuffles through as a slinking jazz number, keen to loosen up the audience with a spacious arrangement hinted at by its titular commas.

A breathy performance from the sensual Olzon steals the show as the leading lady demonstrates yet another string to her bow of impressive vocal diversity. Unfairly criticised for her inability to tackle operatic behemoths such as 'Wishmaster' and 'Phantom of the Opera', Anette could rest assured that on *Imaginaerum*, her characterful charm was demonstrated in abundance. Whilst it all sounds so effortless for Olzon, Tuomas told *Metal Hammer* UK that drummer Jukka sought some professional help in recasting himself as a jazz percussionist:

> You want to challenge yourself to do something that you have absolutely no idea about, and none of us know anything about jazz! Our drummer even had to take some lessons to learn how to use the brush! It all started when I started watching *Twin Peaks* again. I just loved the soundtrack and thought, 'Could we do something like that?', and this is the result.

As if in a fever dream, the familiar Nightwish begin to emerge from the ambient smoke, unable to resist a soaring crescendo. The jazz club caves in around them, collapsing under the weight of the revving guitars and belting Olzon until all that remains is a steady ticking. 'Slow, Love, Slow' might not be a quintessential Nightwish track, but it was a curious glance at what might have been if the group were more taken by warming Parisian Jazz than saunas and Sabbath.

'I Want My Tears Back' 5:08 (Music and lyrics: Tuomas Holopainen)
The black sheep of the album, 'I Want My Tears Back', is more of a sonic bedmate with 'Last of the Wilds' than the primarily symphonic tendencies of *Imaginaerum*. The only song ditching the orchestra and choir completely, it's Troy Donockley at the helm with his multi-faceted skillset, once more making a compelling case to be drafted in as an official member. These shanty elements received a special mention from Tuomas on the album's release, too – 'I love the sea part with the pipes and violin!' – yet another sign that the folkier attributes of Nightwish were here to stay.

'I Want My Tears Back' yearns for a return to the celebration of 'Storytime', a frantic and fruitless search for the awe that had subsided with maturity and age. Even the song's title, though perhaps cloyingly immature to some, retains that voice of the inner child longing for the storybook adventures of youth. The clearest link to Tuomas himself comes with a neatly hidden Disney reference to 'the voice of Mary Costa', the retired actress that provided the voice for Aurora in *Sleeping Beauty*.

The track comes at a crucial time in the sequencing of *Imaginaerum*. Whether charmed or lukewarm by the experimental 'Slow, Love, Slow' or daunted by the more complex 'Scaretale' to follow, the two are wisely separated by the immediate, bounding number. Invited for the full world tour this time around, Troy spearheaded a short folkish detour on the *Imaginaerum* dates, kicked off with 'I Want My Tears Back' and reimagining 'Nemo' along the way. As an unparalleled burst of energy, 'I Want My Tears Back' was secured as a mainstay on setlists across following tours too, one of the few live regulars to stick around for the *Decades* tour in 2018.

'Scaretale' 7:32 (Music and lyrics: Tuomas Holopainen)
'Scaretale' welcomes us back into the loose concept of the album, this time tumbling helplessly into a suffocating nightmare. It amplifies all the elements of 'Ghost River' with unforgettable performances from the vocalists, scaling orchestral peaks and cruelly vanquishing the semblance of hope that had carried us through the haunted waters.

Rather than descending into a pit of anguish as in 'Planet Hell' or 'Master Passion Greed', this time a sense of sadistic fun is retained. If anything, it emphasises the horrors on offer to imagine a smirking audience observing the terror with relish. If the unsettling mix of circus-like cheer juxtaposed with dread-inducing sights rings familiar, Marco spoke to Metal.de about a certain director that served as an influence:

> A lot of people have come to me and said, now that they've heard this thing, it somehow reminds them of Tim Burton and I'm like, that's what we were thinking when we were rehearsing and demoing this thing – that if Tim Burton would make a heavy metal movie, this would actually be a pretty good soundtrack for him.

Tuomas outlined that the song was the Nightwish version of Metallica's colossal beast, 'Enter Sandman'. Though not as career-defining as the US metallers, the influence of a frighteningly vivid childlike imagination ties the two together. For the more scare-adverse Nightwish fan, one main takeaway will be the effortless transition from the grand, symphonic horror of the song's first half into the chilling bazaar of its second, a switch marked by Marco's beguiling 'Ladies and gentlemen, be heartlessly welcome to Cirque De Morgue'. And, of course, who could forget Anette's iconic witchery as she sings of 'burning farms and sque-eeeeeeee-aling pigs'!

'Arabesque' 2:51 (Music: Tuomas Holopainen)

The tie to the movie becomes most apparent on its two instrumental numbers, the first being 'Arabesque', which serves another purpose of cleansing pallets after the onslaught of 'Scaretale'. A continuation of the Egyptian lean of 'Tutankhamen' and 'Sahara', it's a short return to the searing desert heat. The declarative sorna played by Dirk Campbell transports us to the middle east in the first third of the song, though its inclusion is slightly muddled as the instrument originates in Iran, of Persian origin rather than Arabic.

If 'Arabesque' feels somewhat forgettable, it could be down to its key purpose as a movie requirement rather than a necessary part of the *Imaginaerum* album itself. There's certainly an argument that the following track, 'Turn Loose the Mermaids' could have served as the catharsis to 'Scaretale' in its place with a more familiar structure and a gentle approach.

If nothing else, 'Arabesque' is an enjoyable orchestral interlude and whilst it's not a song many would dig out purposely, it's far from a permanent skip. A sole live performance was given during a specially curated set ahead of the *Imaginaerum* movie premiere at Hartwall Arena, elevated to a real visual spectacular by the Polte fire-dancing troupe with footage saved for inclusion on the *Endless Forms Most Beautiful* tour edition.

'Turn Loose the Mermaids' 4:18 (Music and lyrics: Tuomas Holopainen)

Whilst death had thus far been a forbidding force, 'Turn Loose the Mermaids' explores the haunting beauty of loss in a tender acceptance of our inevitable fates. The song has a poignant muse for Tuomas, who explained to *Metal Hammer* UK:

> It was born in the moment when I saw my grandfather die, and my grandmother was giving him the final message. It was one of the most emotional experiences of my life – it was so dark and beautiful at the same time. I had to make a song about it – the last thing she did was check his teeth, warm his toes, and then [say] 'Good journey, my love, see you soon'. She was 93 back then, and 15 minutes after, he died. I'd never seen a dead person before, and it was an emotional moment, so I wanted to do a song about it. The album's all about life and the power and beauty of imagination, and I thought that we needed to include the final chapter of life, which is death.

'Turn Loose the Mermaids' is a continuation of another recurrent theme in the Nightwish catalogue – a tender receiving of death, later explored in some depth on the following *Endless Forms Most Beautiful* record. The lyrics draw primarily on reality ('I checked your teeth and warmed your toes') but peppers a figurative enchantment ('a child holding on to the magic of birth and awe') and, fittingly for life's reflective final chapter, recalls lyrics from other *Imaginaerum* compositions ('at the end of the river…', 'the mermaids you turned loose brought back your tears').

The music here is sparse, stripped back and warming beneath Anette's crystalline voice. As the group so often employ, an ascending crescendo awaits with the final reprise of the chorus, bringing the song to a melodious gallop that the songwriter compares to a 'spaghetti western'. Despite a warm reception from fans, the endless battle for setlist ballad spots has unfortunately robbed 'Turn Loose the Mermaids' of its chance of a live outing thus far.

'Rest Calm' 7:00 (Music and lyrics: Tuomas Holopainen)

Lifting the title of 'Turn Loose the Mermaids' from the My Dying Bride album *Turn Loose the Swans*, it was the music of the English metal band that inspired the doomy undertones of 'Rest Calm'. Once again, the song tackles loss, but rather than the griever, we are now asked to ponder our own deaths. It is no surprise when Tuomas hopes for an oceanic passing, though this time more realistically asking to 'die in a seaside hotel' rather than a crashing corpse forgotten to the waves. 'Rest Calm' is also more human in its confession of fear as Marco sings to his loved ones to 'stay by my side until it all goes dark forever'.

These anxious moments are intermittent, the core of the song revealing itself with a slower, lapping chorus that sounds meditative in its repetition. 'Rest Calm' is a song concerned with a fervent preservation of cherished recollections, the children's choir reprising to give yet more resonance to the power of memories. Tuomas underlined the premise upon the album's announcement – 'the sweetness of my own past is a bottomless chest of comfort and inspiration' – on *Imaginaerum* and across Nightwish's entire discography, the songwriter's memories are safeguarded as part of the band's enduring legacy.

'Rest Calm' had an unforeseen significance for Anette Olzon as it was performed with her for the first and last time at the fateful Salt Lake City show, which proved to be her last as a member of Nightwish. The only other setlist inclusion was a night earlier when Marco took solo vocal duties during the infamous show cobbled together alongside one-night vocalists Elize Ryd and Alissa White-Gluz.

'The Crow, The Owl and the Dove' 4:07 (Music: Marco Hietala, lyrics: Tuomas Holopainen)

'Rather than love, than money, than fame, give me Truth' is the Thoreau quote that Tuomas used to describe 'The Crow, The Owl and the Dove' ahead of the album's release. He was even more forthcoming with his muse when speaking to *Metal Hammer* UK:

> I have to admit it's a bit of a rip-off because I'm a big fan of Henry David Thoreau, the poet from the 19th Century. I read his book *Walden*, where he said, 'I don't care about the love, the beauty, the pride or anything, just give me the truth. I thought there was a big philosophy behind that, and I started to think I could make a song about it. The crowd represents pride, the owl wisdom and the dove love and peace.

Calling it a rip-off feels a little harsh, but the song does stick loyally to Thoreau's words, recasting them as the main hook of the second single release from *Imaginaerum*. The wise owl might have been lifted from Thoreau's inspiration, but it was also something of a motif across Nightwish records too, particularly on the *Oceanborn* album cover and single releases and re-emerging across numerous merchandise items.

As well as the three titular birds – the proud crow, the wise owl, and the benevolent dove – the song also observes a graceful swan. As each is praised in turn, the lyrics insist that the only trait that matters is truth. It's a sobering reminder in an album that is focused on imagination and creative thinking, giving *Imaginaerum* a firm grounding in reality. It's not just truth that Anette sings in longing for either, after all, it wouldn't be a Nightwish album without pining at least once for lost innocence.

As the second and final single release from *Imaginaerum*, the CD release included the long-awaited cover of 'The Heart Asks Pleasure First' as well as an instrumental of both songs. A slightly shorter cut of the song was also edited and promoted via a fan video competition, asking enthusiastic Nightwish listeners to have a go at putting together their own visual accompaniment for the song. The competition was eventually won by Portuguese Pedro Calvo, who reflected back on his animated video to The Podcast and the Pendulum:

This can come down from personal interpretation, which I strongly defend... but I think it's about wanting to transcend the things that come and go and focus on the truth... the birds represent the things that can distract us from the truth but the truth is always there and doesn't change.

The bridge is left to Troy Donockley and his incantations: 'Gar tuht river, ger te rheged', underscored by his whistles and earthy pipes. Roughly translated as an invitation to follow the river to reach the old north kingdom of Rheged, it's not clear whether the destination offered either innocence or truth, but it certainly gave a convincing clue that Troy would soon become an official Nightwish member.

'Last Ride of the Day' 4:30 (Music and lyrics: Tuomas Holopainen)
Running with the cliché of an emotional rollercoaster, 'Last Ride of the Day' is the electrifying highlight of *Imaginaerum*. If 'Rest Calm' and 'Turn Loose the Mermaids' sang of our final rest, this is life flashing before our eyes. Embodying every element of the cinematic Nightwish sound, it boasts driving riffs, choral bursts and an orchestral steer that envelops the entire ride; it's easy to see why it has become an adored Nightwish classic.

We open the second verse with the telling lyric 'wake up, dead boy – enter adventureland', Tuomas' distancing himself from the woeful self-pity of old and reminding himself to look for the abounding magic in the 'carnival of life'. The takeaway lyric comes in the chorus, a harsh truth wrapped in the songwriter's usual poetry – 'it's hard to light a candle, easy to curse the dark instead'; the time for commiseration has passed and 'Last Ride of the Day' is all too happy to host an enthralling procession over its remains.

Its flagrant celebration of life helped the song reach unexpected places. Elements of 'Last Ride of the Day' were the world's first taste of *Imaginaerum* as it was remixed by DJ Orkidea to become a completely redesigned 'Kiteen Pallo', the entrance music for the Finnish Pesäpallo team of the same name. In the 2016 Olympic summer games, the song was also used to soundtrack a jaw-dropping performance from the Australian synchronised swimming team, though sadly not quite enough to score a medal.

'Last Ride of the Day' is another song particularly tied to the movie in which the character of Thomas (how on earth did they come up with that name?) makes his grand realisation onboard a rapid rollercoaster ride. It's a particularly arresting scene from the film, with the song's punchy reprise carrying the viewer through the disjointed journey, detouring at many points to revisit prominent memories. The thrills are recreated on the live scene too, with a twisting, turning first-person video of the riotous rollercoaster ride playing behind the group. Needless to say, the song and the exhilarating staging have retained a worthy presence on setlists across all tours since.

The song's euphoric message, albeit tinged with a healthy dose of realism, entwines with the majesty of the orchestra that has daunted, terrified and thrilled us on our journey. 'Last Ride of the Day' serves as an honorary closer for the record since the following 'Song of Myself' is less strict in its movie-companion responsibilities and 'Imaginaerum' rolls the story's credits. As the setlist closer on *Imaginaerum* tour dates, it was also the last song performed by Nightwish with Anette as vocalist; a bittersweet but appropriate final duet for a group of individuals that had taken their own turbulent journey together.

'Song of Myself' (i. 'From a Dusty Bookshelf', ii. 'All That Great Heart Lying Still', iii. 'Piano Black', iv. 'Love') 13:30 (Music and lyrics: Tuomas Holopainen)

The human journey had underscored all the songs of the album so far, if slightly obscured at times by the storytime steer, the theme park imagery, and Tuomas' usual poetic license. For 'Song of Myself', only the latter remains and even that begins to ebb away by the song's affecting final part. Taking its title from Walt Whitman's 52-part poem, 'Song of Myself' is Tuomas' unashamed tribute to the writer, as he commented of the song: 'our homage and version of Walt Whitman`s transcendental celebration of life and existence, delving deep into a personal catharsis'.

Initially, it's not too far apart from the bombast we come to expect from Nightwish. The thirteen-and-a-half-minute runtime may attract attention, but there's a comfortable familiarity in the explosive 'From a Dusty Bookshelf', which begins the transition from the storybook to the storyteller. 'All That Great Heart Lying Still' is the melodic heart of the epic, introducing a choral refrain that sticks around for a welcome reprise. Its lyrics again recall the misery of the dead boy and the cathartic freedom that comes with imagination. It's a satisfying hark back to the album as a whole, too, when Anette sings of 'storytime and the river ghosts, of mermaids, of Whitman's and the ride'.

Next up, 'Piano Black' is a brief, downbeat departure that returns to the moodier tones of 'Rest Calm', juxtaposing the menacing black sky with the cleansing waters beneath. Notes of 'rusting keys without a door' find a composer not only struggling with a creative block but seeping into a depressive state at the loss of his vital escapism. 'Piano Black' finds the songwriter at a low ebb – the perfect time to reflect on the cleansing realities of the prolonged final chapter, 'Love'.

Given its title, 'Love' doesn't suggest much of the harsh truths it unpacks, making the admissions all the more powerful. Unquestionably the most divisive element of the song, the spoken word poem takes in a huge 23 stanzas and cares little for brevity, though each voice delivers only a snapshot of a moment. It's a capture of life in its entirety – the shame of loneliness, the recognition of hypocrisy, a search for a balanced life – and a host of speakers, each bringing their own experience into the fold. Rather than nudge away at one theme, 'Love' opens the song up to the diversity of our minds, our observations and our own individual concerns.

The final section boasts plenty of uncredited speakers, mostly pulled from the band's inner circles, as Marco told Metal.de:

> Troy [Donockley] is speaking, Pip [Williams] is speaking, and then there are people that we know, friends, family members and all that… I asked my sons to do a couple of lines together, and my father. None of the characters is me. I mean none of us, the band, are there at the end, in that long recitation.

Love it or hate it, it's the spoken poem that pulls 'Song of Myself' away from any lazy comparisons to other Nightwish epics and stamps it with its own USP. The divisive ending meant a more lukewarm reception for the song upon release, many fans expecting a final swell from the lengthy composition rather than a quiet drifting into silence. Wisely recognising that the recitation wouldn't translate live, performances of 'Song of Myself' draw to a close after the meditative 'Piano Black'. It does sacrifice a sizeable chunk of the song's magic, winding down on a melancholic note rather than the thought-provoking 'Love', but is a fair compromise to help recreate the song onstage, employing a technique that would also be rehashed for the next album's epic.

'Imaginaerum' 6:18 (Music: Tuomas Holopainen, Arrangement: Pip Williams)

Defining the track on the band's website, Tuomas wrote: 'Thank you for sharing the ride and we hope to welcome you back soon. The stage is lit, and the Magnificent Play is beginning...' Just as on 'The Poet and the Pendulum', the beginning is announced at the last moment, a rebirth of realisation. Fresh from the observations of 'Song of Myself', the imploration of 'Last Ride of the Day' and the comfort of 'Turn Loose the Mermaids', we are reintroduced to our realities and challenged to appreciate the everyday with eyes wide open.

Recapping the album's expansive voyage, 'Imaginaerum' is an instrumental soundtrack intended for the movie credits. It's a medley arranged completely by collaborator Pip Williams, using the orchestral elements of the album's tracks; each one is reprised in tracklist order, omitting 'I Want My Tears Back' due to its lack of orchestra.

The 'Imaginaerum' outro is an appropriate segue into the *Imaginaerum: The Score* release, which dropped a year later. The score draws on the album's orchestral arrangements -many melodies and segments instantly recognisable for keen-eared fans – and cuts out the vast majority of lyrics save for 'Deeper Down', which repurposes the verses from 'The Crow, The Owl and The Dove'. As *Imaginaerum* was the band's first release without any original B-sides or bonus tracks – 'The Heart Asks Pleasure First' being both a cover and recorded during the *Dark Passion Play* sessions – the score is an appeasing offering for Nightwish loyalists, providing plenty of musical easter eggs to uncover.

The score celebrates what became of the *Imaginaerum* movie, which was eventually premiered in November 2012. Though not quite as successful as the storming Nightwish record that preceded it, it's impossible to uncouple the album and the film; still, Tuomas admitted to *Metal Hammer* that the original scope for the album's release was very different:

> Back in 2007, I started to wonder what we could do after *Dark Passion Play*. I had the idea of combining a movie with an album: I would write maybe 12 or 13 songs and we would film a short movie for all of them. It would be a double CD; an audio disc would contain the songs and there would also be a DVD. That was the seed of my idea. There would be no professional actors, no dialogue, no plot or storyline; only the music videos for the songs. So I introduced my idea to Stobe Harju, the director of the video for 'The Islander'. He thought it was excellent, saying that nobody had done anything like it before. He went a stage further still. He suggested that we make a full-length drama movie that would condense those songs' ideas of mine into the script. I'm not going to try and steal the glory for that: it was 100 per cent Stobe's idea to have an old man sitting back and looking over his past life.

Though Nightwish almost became the pioneers, Beyoncé would popularise the concept of a visual album only a few years later with her self-titled release. No time for regrets, successfully scaling a full-length feature in support of a record was a momentous task and fulfilled a lifelong ambition for Holopainen.

'Show Me How to Die' (Live Cover) (Music and lyrics: Anton Kabanen)
Now for something quite niche indeed. A backstage clip of Nightwish delivering a guitar-strumming, seat-slapping minute of 'Show Me How to Die' by Battle Beast gave a charming glimpse into happier times on the ill-fated *Imaginaerum* tour. The song was reprised onstage for the final date of the tour's first European leg as a fond farewell to their fellow Finns who had supported during the jaunt. Rather than a rehearsed rendition, the few fan-recorded live clips of 'Show Me How to Die' reveal another side of the group, spontaneous and silly, despite the more serious and considered image they are often tarred with.

'The Mug of Brown Ale' (Live Cover) (Traditional)
Foot-stomping Irish traditional 'The Mug of Brown Ale' was a chance for guest Troy Donockley to prove that he could offer more than a sombre backing to 'The Islander' and other acoustic-led ballads. Its first recorded performance was at the Denver show in which Anette was taken to hospital. As time-fillers go, 'The Mug of Brown Ale' proved a winner – remaining as an extended intro to 'Over the Hills and Far Away' for the remainder of the tour dates and being reprised again on the Nightwish cruise in 2015.

'Christmas Song for a Lonely Documentarist' 3:33 (Uncredited)
Tucked away on the Showtime, Storytime live release, this tongue-in-cheek ode was dedicated to Finnish director and regular collaborator Ville Lipiäinen. The simple toe-tapper takes heed from traditional acoustic storytelling ("Oh hear me ye good people, come and lend me your ear!") to share the woes of documenting Nightwish's hectic Imaginaerum world tour. The rockstar clichés are ticked off with room service threats and TVs in questionable locations, but it's the pure camaraderie that brings some festive warmth to the silliness.

Endless Forms Most Beautiful (2015)

Personnel:
Floor Jansen: vocals
Kai Hahto: drums
Marco Hietala: bass, vocals, acoustic guitars
Tuomas Holopainen: keys, piano
Emppu Vuorinen: guitars
Troy Donockley: bodhran, uilleann pipes, low whistles, bouzouki, vocals
London Philharmonic (credited as the Orchestre de Grandeur): orchestra
Pip Williams: orchestra and choir arrangements
James Shearman: conductor
Steve Price: orchestra engineer
Jeremy Murphy: orchestra engineer assistant
Metro Voices and Young Musicians London: choirs
Jenny O'Grady: choirmaster (Metro Voices choir), choral coordinator (Young Musicians London Choir)
Lynda Richardson: choirmaster (Young Musicians London choir)
Professor Richard Dawkins: spoken word ('Shudder Before the Beautiful', 'The Greatest Show On Earth')
Jussi Tegelman: soundscapes, musical echoes ('The Greatest Show on Earth')
Francesca Lupica: cosmic beam experience ('The Greatest Show on Earth')
Recorded between August and October 2014 by Mikko Karmila and Tero Kinnunen
Recorded at Petrax Studio, Angel Studios and Röskö Campsite
Richard Dawkins recordings by Michael Taylor at Hats off Studios
Arranged by Tuomas Holopainen, Jukka Nevalainen, Marco Hietala and Emppu Vuorinen, Floor Jansen, Kai Hahto, Troy Donockley
Mixed by Mikko Karmila at Finnvox Studios between October and December 2014
Engineered by Mikko Karmila and Tero Kinnunen
Produced by Tuomas Holopainen
Mika Jussila: mastering
Ville Juurikkala: band photography
Janne Pitkänen (ToxicAngel): album artwork
Gina Pitkänen: album artwork

With Floor Jansen at the helm, Nightwish remerged as something of a symphonic metal supergroup. The usual anticipation for a new studio record was exceeded as keen After Forever and ReVamp fans pondered just how Tuomas would make use of Jansen's masterful vocal capabilities. Perhaps keen to curb expectations, when 'Élan' dropped in February 2015 a more restrained Nightwish emerged. According to Tuomas, the song was 'giving out a little taste, but revealing very little of the actual journey of grandeur to come' and curiously, it was actually the pipes of fellow newbie Troy Donockley that had the most significant presence on the lead single.

'Élan' proved to be a rocky start for the album. The song leaked online a few days early, resulting in a frustrated Nightwish naming and shaming a distributor on their Facebook account. Whether succumbing to the leaks or waiting for the official release a few days later, fans expecting the usual more-is-more approach were torn, though soon placated by a confirmation that Nightwish's most ambitious epic to date was to be the dominating finale of the forthcoming record.

A better taste for the grandiose *Endless Forms Most Beautiful* was the B-side to 'Élan', a symphonic romp that years earlier would have been a shoo-in for a single release. As its name indicates, 'Sagan' was a tribute to the astronomer and author Carl Sagan with lyrics declaring 'woe to all who stop at the horizon', another hint that grander things were to come on the parent album.

The line-up was to transform once again with drummer Jukka Nevalainen's insomnia demanding he step down from his duties behind the kit. Nevalainen would still play a role behind the scenes but admitted that he could no longer muster 'the precision that the music deserves', yielding his drumming duties to Wintersun's Kai Hahto ahead of the album's release date.

When *Endless Forms Most Beautiful* dropped in March 2015, the triptych of muses was complete: Whitman's awe remained, the work of Sagan inspired and, perhaps most crucially, Charles Darwin's theory of evolution became the centrepiece of the record, lending the album its title. Making the headlines at the time of release was the contribution from revered evolutionary biologist Richard Dawkins, certainly not the type of guest artist expected on a metal record. After a short spoken-word introduction, Dawkins returned to elevate the album closer 'The Greatest Show on Earth', reciting from his 2000 book *Unweaving the Rainbow*:

> We are going to die, and that makes us the lucky ones. Most people are never going to die because they are never going to be born. The potential people who could have been here in my place but who will in fact, never see the light of day outnumber the sand grains of Arabia. Certainly, those unborn ghosts include greater poets than Keats, scientists greater than Newton. We know this because the set of possible people allowed by our DNA so massively exceeds the set of actual people. In the teeth of these stupefying odds, it is you and I, in our ordinariness, that are here. We privileged few, who won the lottery of birth against all odds, how dare we whine at our inevitable return to that prior state from which the vast majority have never stirred?

There was simply no better way to express the intention of the record and no better scientist to collaborate on the task. *Endless Forms Most Beautiful* challenged listeners to consider that a world without a God or religion can still evoke abounding wonder. It followed in the footsteps of *Imaginaerum* and paid tribute to the everyday, honouring family on 'Our Decades in the

Sun', mother earth in 'My Walden' and 'Alpenglow' and at once cherishing our individual paths ('Élan') and the united journey of mankind ('The Greatest Show on Earth').

Following their viral success, the demand to see Nightwish live was like never before. This culminated in yet another recording, *Vehicle of Spirit*, which immortalised a headlining show at Wembley arena (the first Finnish band ever to do so) featuring Richard Dawkins himself. A second DVD also included a full show from Tampere recorded months earlier. Whilst it didn't manage to reach the dizzying heights of *Showtime, Storytime*, the release commemorated the *Endless Forms Most Beautiful* world tour, which saw 150 shows worldwide before embarking on the 80+ dates of the *Decades* tour just two years later. Twenty years into their career, Nightwish's campfire compositions were dominating the world stage and not even influential Scientists could refute their appeal.

'Shudder Before the Beautiful' 6:30 (Music and lyrics: Tuomas Holopainen)

The theme of *Endless Forms Most Beautiful* is made apparent from the off: 'a species from the veil walks in wander in search of the source of the tale'. From silence emerges a brief and commanding quote from Richard Dawkins, trailed by a tinkering string section that soon builds to a wall of heavy, orchestral depth. The song transports us to the stars, overlooking the celestial island of earth – the lead player in the album's concept.

From Floor's first line, the song also digs deep within the band's own lore as the oceanborn are finally awoken to this spellbinding existence. Tuomas pulls himself out of his imaginary haven and nostalgic rapture, opening his eyes on the 'sumptuous planet' that Dawkins reveres at many points across the record. 'Shudder Before the Beautiful' is not only an ideal opener for the way it lends itself to the concept, but also the perfect way to draw a line between the Nightwish of old and the new, conscious mindset that permeated the compositions. Commenting to *Spazio Rock*, Tuomas said:

> ...the song reminds me heavily of the songs from *Once,* maybe even *Oceanborn*. For the first time in like 15 years, we have this keyboard-guitar battle going on there, so it's really old-school Nightwish.

This brief return to the power metal leanings of *Wishmaster* and *Oceanborn* appears as a duelling pair of solos between Emppu and Tuomas, offering an almost space opera sound akin to Arjen Lucassen's Ayreon and Star One projects. The chorus and main refrain are delightfully familiar fare, though – bombastic, euphoric, and employing the classic key change to raise the roof for final reprises.

Between the *Oceanborn* throwbacks and the unexpected Richard Dawkins cameo, it's Floor Jansen's voice that will have demanded the immediate focus on first listens. With *Endless Forms Most Beautiful* marking her first studio release as Nightwish vocalist, expectations were stratospheric from an audience that were well aware of Floor's exceptional skillset. On the album's opener, it's down to Jansen alone to captain the interstellar ship and though it isn't the time for showboating, the strength of her conviction in the chorus contrasted with a gentle, mystified delivery in the verses made clear that Floor was able to deliver exactly what the song needed.

'Weak Fantasy' 5:25 (Music and lyrics: Marco Hietala and Tuomas Holopainen)

Endless Forms Most Beautiful is a record that stands firm in its resolve of science over religion and the proudly secular nature of the release just couldn't pass without an exploration and criticism of the prescriptive, organised latter. It makes sense, too, for an album so evangelically enchanted by the everyday miracle of life; there's an underlying urge on 'Weak Fantasy' to turn away from any blind belief that obscures the appreciation of our remarkable evolution.

'Weak Fantasy' doesn't pull any punches with its intent – 'he loves you dwelling in fear and sin' Floor mocks, Marco later succinctly criticising the violent impact of stubborn religious belief: 'from words into war of the worlds'. Fresh from the theme of the *Imaginaerum* album, a faint glimmer of admiration at the stories that have captured millions is evident throughout, religious texts described as 'tribal poetry' and the admission of 'a storytelling breed are we'. It's a shift for Tuomas lyrically after leaning on religious imagery and iconography since the *Angels Fall First* days; he was asked by Andrew Marlowe-Cremedas to discuss this in a fan Q&A:

> The album's thematics are heavily influenced by science, and beauty of the natural world and our rare existence, yes. Religions are fascinating, though, and their history and imagery are inspiring tools for creating art. I became a freethinker (secularist, atheist, agnostic... whatever, it's all semantics) after realising I have a (loose) belief in something I know nothing about. I suppose the biggest realisation came from the fact that out of the 3,500 existing religions in the world today, I happened to lucky enough be born to the single correct one...?! I felt a deeply uncomfortable twitch of arrogance. That, and also, actually reading some of that 'Good Book' made quite the difference. I'm happy to stand before the big questions and say, 'I don't know', until we know better. And to know better, science, backed up by reason and evidence is the only way.

The song elevates tremendously from an unexpected middle eight where an acoustic passage occurs in amongst the angst. It's a brief, unsettling calm before the fist-punching symphonic blasts that underscore Marco's first vocal contribution to the album, a fitting place for him to take the spotlight as he told *Louder Sound* about the song's composition:

> This is a combination of an interesting metal song with a few interesting parts that dabble in Celtic folk with the acoustic guitars… I actually wrote the acoustic guitar part in the middle of this song, and I think it provides a nice dynamic difference... It's also got a nice rhythmic structure that we haven't really done that much before, and it's another good one to do live.

Marco wasn't wrong – on the *Endless Forms Most Beautiful* tour, the song was a riotous highlight. The bassist drafted in his multi-necked guitar to accompany Troy in the acoustic segment before the final chorus saw domineering bursts of smoke shot from behind the group, rendering them as elusive silhouettes not too dissimilar from the fantasy deities that the song critiques.

'Élan' 4:45 (Music and lyrics: Tuomas Holopainen)
Defined as a vigorous enthusiasm, 'Élan' is an apt title for *Endless Forms Most Beautiful*'s charming lead single. It is remarkably understated for a Nightwish track, showcasing more of Troy Donockley's influence on the band than Floor's vocals or their usual bombast. 'Élan' readied listeners for an evolved sound and, when experienced in the sequenced order of the album tracklist, strode confidently away from the usual Nightwish approach. Initially, only Marco and Troy's choice for lead single, Jukka shared in the book *We Were Here* that the rest were soon convinced: 'six persons can rarely agree on everything but in the end 'Élan' was a unanimous choice'.

The change wasn't completely unforeseen. Troy's invitation to join the band, the growing prominence of folkier influences and Tuomas and Troy's burgeoning Celtic-inspired side project Auri were all clues that spiralling orchestrals were no longer the only signature to Nightwish's sound. Yet, following the enormity of *Imaginaerum*, the response to the single was divisive – fears of a complete symphonic dropout doused the upcoming album in unnecessary apprehension. Whether it was the relief that *Endless Forms Most Beautiful* still offered the expected splendour or simply a growing fondness towards 'Élan' over time, the song's roaring live reception and a deserved place as a setlist mainstay wiped all memory of those initial dissenting responses. One of the song's most vocal fans was *Interview with the Vampire* writer Anne Rice who shared the official video upon release, rebuking her tendency as a latecomer to 'great groups' such as Nightwish.

Thematically, 'Élan' presented the celebratory heart of *Endless Forms Most Beautiful* and insisted that an album rooted in science need not be a sterile, emotionless venture. One of Nightwish's most striking single sleeves, the single art reinforced the liberation of the album's theme – a Peter Pan-esque silhouette leaping from a cliff into an inviting unknown. With CD singles quickly becoming a thing of the past, an exclusive B-side was unveiled to sweeten the deal in 'Sagan' and an alternate version and radio edit of 'Élan' rounded the package out, leading to another top three hit in Finland.

As urban explorers, the band traversed numerous abandoned locations to film the video for 'Élan', culminating in the joyous finale in which the video's charismatic Finnish actors dance in exuberant festivities as the band play. A unique setting was sourced for each member, as well as the array of famous Finnish faces, making it one of the most dynamic videos in the band's history – it also marked the final role of noted Finnish actor Antti Litja who sadly passed away shortly after the filming.

'Yours is an Empty Hope' 5:34 (Music: Tuomas Holopainen, lyrics: Tuomas Holopainen and Marco Hietala)

Almost missing out on a tracklist spot to eventual B-side 'Sagan', 'Yours is an Empty Hope' sandwiches the gentler 'Élan' between two of the album's darkest moments. It's a sequencing dream, underlining the album's dynamism which continues into yet another contrasting follow-up in 'Our Decades in the Sun'. Approaching the album holistically was the reason for its inclusion – Tuomas commenting that the album needed just a little more heaviness, something this track was more than capable of injecting.

A remarkable similarity to 'Dark Chest of Wonders' in the song's opening riffs soon descends where the *Once* opener had soared, readying the listener for a callous reprimand. Floor's sarcastic verses make clear that unwarranted demands and opinions wash right over her whilst Marco booms the title lyric on repeat in the chorus. Not too distant from the purging 'Master Passion Greed', it's almost startling when the band take up their swords and march into conflict, listeners much more familiar with the self-loathing of 'Slaying the Dreamer' than the admonishing of 'Yours Is an Empty Hope'.

It's a departure from the album's theme, clearly born of immense frustration; the mention of 'screen names' suggests that ever-vocal online trolls could be the muse for the merciless tirade. Certainly, journalists and commenters alike had plenty to say about Olzon's departure from the group years before – 'Yours is an Empty Hope' makes clear that any unsolicited input into personal band matters has been, and will continue to be, firmly rebuffed.

'Our Decades in the Sun' 6:37 (Music: Marco Hietala, Tuomas Holopainen, lyrics: Tuomas Holopainen)

'Our Decades in the Sun' is a powerful tribute to family, dedicated to the band's parents and prompting plenty of emotions in the rehearsals and recording sessions. It was shortly after saying goodbye to her parents, both of whom had made a trip to visit her in Finland, that Floor was tasked with the recording session. The stirring emotion that emanated from her vocal performance was recalled by Marco in the book *We Were Here* by Timo Isoaho:

> We were waiting in the control room for Floor to start singing the first verse of 'Our Decades in the Sun'. There was not a peep, and then we heard

> something. It was quiet sobbing. Recording the vocals for 'Decades' was one of the most memorable moments of the whole session. The lyrics are just so damn meaningful and emotional.

The children's choir from *Imaginaerum* gently ebb to Floor's opening line, making clear the song's muse: 'I climbed off your back not so long ago'. It seeps through the journey of a lifelong relationship, the never-ending need for a parent's love and the miraculous wonder of their benevolence. In keeping with the album's theme, the song doesn't fear death – it closes with a touching promise and reflection: 'our walk has been sublime… one day we'll meet on that shore again'. Still, the song dedicates over two minutes in drawing out that inevitable end with distant vocalisations from Marco and Floor and Troy's evocative low whistles, a subtle reminder that these losses remain a challenging thing to accept, though the memories endure long after the grief.

It's the simpler, quieter moments that are often the hardest to perfect and Tuomas confirmed as much to *Spazio Rock*, describing it as 'maybe the most difficult song to put together because it is so delicate, so intimate' When it came to such cathartic compositions, a persistent worry around Floor Jansen's creative urges has also been mentioned on numerous occasions. As lead songwriter in After Forever, Revamp and her solo releases, fans ponder if the vocalist will remain content as merely an interpreter of Tuomas' work. At the time, at least, Jansen commented to *Uber Rock* about her contentment:

> I am the voice, the translator of these words and emotions, and I feel honoured. I let it transmit through me, but he is the maestro and it's due to his brilliance that this band is what it is.

It's in Jansen's solo ventures that 'Our Decades in the Sun' received a special tribute. During Floor's time on the Dutch TV series *Beste Zangers*, in which artists reinterpret one another's songs in intimate performances, eventual winner Samantha Steenwijk chose to translate the heartfelt number into Dutch in honour of Jansen, retitling it as 'Jij zit voor altijd in mij' or 'You are Forever in Me'. On her subsequent Dutch tour, Floor herself gave the Nightwish song its live debut as part of a setlist that honoured both her time on *Beste Zangers* and her career to date.

'My Walden' 4:38 (Music: Tuomas Holopainen, Marco Hietala, lyrics: Tuomas Holopainen)

Labelled as a continuation of 'I Want My Tears Back', Troy is again pushed to the musical frontline, even offering his vocals to the Welsh-language intro that Floor loosely harks back to later in English. 'My Walden' is a lot more progressive than its straight-forward *Imaginaerum* sibling, drifting away from the celebratory folksong after only two minutes and dropping the tempo for Troy's enchanting whistles to take centre stage atop a hypnotic acoustic loop.

'My Walden' bubbles with optimism as it imagines a utopian world, rife with Holopainen's usual nods to nature ('The sound of mist, smell of moss-grown woods') and other flights of fancy (the chocolate shop referenced inspired by a British trip with Troy). The title is inspired by the book *Walden* by Henry David Thoreau, a documentation of the author's self-imposed solitude over the course of two years, during which he lived in a self-built cabin and pondered true fulfilment. *Sea of Tranquility* drew on the final reflective lyric – 'I do not wish to evade the world, but I will forever build my own' – to which Tuomas responded:

> That's the whole essence of the song and that's how I felt when I read *Walden* for the first time, too. I, as a person, am very optimistic. I just can't take the 'this world sucks', 'everything's dark and rotten', 'I just want to escape'. The world is a beautiful place. It's what we make of it. That's why I don't want to evade the world. It's beautiful. But I will still have my Walden, my own Walden. Everybody should. Stop the complaining and do something about it, to put it bluntly. I know it's not so easy for everybody...

The Walden-like writing sessions took place, as they always do, in a tucked-away campsite, with Tuomas bringing forth a strong foundation of demos for the band to rehearse and refine. For the first time in Nightwish's history, their vocalist insisted on attending the sessions alongside the other members, Floor commenting to *DPRP*: 'For the first time Tuomas sat in the studio with a singer to try different ways of singing and he liked that approach very much. For example, 'My Walden' has changed dramatically because of our being in the studio all together'. It was also a crucial show of unity from the off, Floor determined to solidify her role in the group. All members, including Jansen, were credited with these final album arrangements in the *Endless Forms Most Beautiful* booklet.

From the ashes of the dying market of physical single releases, a growing support of Record Store Day had emerged; these events saw the release of vinyl and special editions to celebrate and support independent record shops and were marked by Nightwish in 2016 with the exclusive 'My Walden' vinyls in green and gold. *Endless Forms Most Beautiful*'s sole bonus track already having been milked for all it was worth, 'My Walden' was instead padded out with a spectral offering – live versions of 'Ghost River' and 'Ghost Love Score', both lifted from *Showtime, Storytime*.

'Endless Forms Most Beautiful' 5:07 (Music and lyrics: Tuomas Holopainen)

Curiously, of all the songs on the album – one of the least essential cuts is the album's second single and title track. 'Endless Forms Most Beautiful' was expected by the band to be a fan favourite, Marco commenting in the

We Were Here book: 'I was sometimes surprised by the crowd reaction to new songs. The title track didn't seem to go down so well, although we had thought it would be a sure-fire live favourite'. Neither as fierce as the likes of 'Weak Fantasy' nor as emotive or resonant as 'Élan', the title track occupied a less impactful middle ground. Launching immediately into a driving synth and drum intro, unleashed chugging riffs steer towards the singalong chorus. Not a poor effort by any means, but unable to muster up much that isn't done better elsewhere.

The song is heavily inspired by Richard Dawkins' book *The Ancestor's Tale: A Pilgrimage to the Dawn of Life,* with the titular phrase itself taken from a Charles Darwin quote from *The Origin of Species* which Dawkins later recites during the album's final track, 'The Greatest Show on Earth':

> There is grandeur in this view of life, with its several powers, having been originally breathed into a few forms or into one; and that, whilst this planet has gone cycling on according to the fixed law of gravity, from so simple a beginning Endless Forms Most Beautiful and wonderful have been, and are being, evolved.

The lyrics are the main takeaway of the track; personifying the nucleus-enveloped eukaryote organisms, diving into the super-ocean of Panthalassa and documenting the extinct Tiktaalik fish, which changes the course of evolution by venturing onto the land. Twisting within the references of evolutionary pivots, the chorus refrain encourages us with great enthusiasm to be 'alive, aware, in awe before the grandeur of it all', witnesses to the grand show that surrounds us.

It could be argued that 'Endless Forms Most Beautiful' was a wise thematic choice for a single, even if the song itself wasn't nearly as effectual as the soaring 'Alpenglow' or 'Weak Fantasy'. The promotional clip was comprised of a band performance overlayed with lyrics, having been shot during the same sessions as 'Élan' and a remarkably similar single package was unveiled. A radio edit shaving off a minute of runtime, an alternative version (as on 'Élan', these alternates were reimagined by *Imaginaerum* score collaborator Petri Alanko) and even the return of the album's sole B-side 'Sagan', this time in its instrumental guise.

'Edema Ruh' 5:14 (Music and lyrics: Tuomas Holopainen)

'Edema Ruh' is an unashamed celebration of what Nightwish had become; looking back on the *Oceanborn* days when Tuomas began to dream that a life in music could be a reality, this song rebrands Nightwish as the titular Edema Ruh, a travelling band of musicians and entertainers as taken from the book *The Name of the Wind* by US author Patrick Rothfuss. It's a satisfying culmination of the ambitions outlined on *Oceanborn* B-side 'Nightquest' way back in 1998, the fantasy having melded into actuality.

It's interesting to think that 'Edema Ruh' was very seriously considered as a single choice. Although it never got the treatment in the end, in the context of the album in its entirety, the song simply doesn't stand out as much as other tracks. If 'Élan' was considered too out-of-the-box, surely 'Edema Ruh' would have been critiqued for its contrastingly safe sound. There was now an expectation that a Nightwish album would cram in plenty of surprises – indeed a creeping progressive influence was taking hold too – and in this respect, 'Edema Ruh' served well as a comforting, easy listen in amongst the experimentation. Tasked with promoting a highly anticipated album, however, it likely wouldn't have shone quite as well under the glare of the unforgiving spotlight. A beefed-up version was teased in the band's *We Were Here* book, but it's not clarified whether this audio makeover was used for the final album cut or existed only as an unreleased single edit.

The group must have had a dramatic change of heart after the album's release, too, since 'Edema Ruh' has rarely featured in setlists for the *Endless Forms Most Beautiful* world tour. On occasion, it has been dug out, receiving its live debut in acoustic form on the Nightwish cruise in 2015, then eventually a full band debut during December 2015 in Munich. From then on, the track has had a meagre seven outings – 'Élan', by comparison, can boast a remarkable 261. It certainly seemed the right choice was made when it came to the lead single.

'Alpenglow' 4:45 (Music and lyrics: Tuomas Holopainen)

Death: on *Once*, a mournful realisation, on *Dark Passion Play*, a necessary catharsis and on *Endless Forms Most Beautiful*, a miraculous return to the life-giving earth. It isn't often that a song about the daunting final rest manages to be so boundlessly optimistic, but 'Alpenglow' underlines a clear evolution in Tuomas' own views of existence and expiration. The title refers to a phenomenon in which a striking reddish glow is visible near the horizon, the song revelling in our remains eventually becoming one with the very same wonder-filled planet.

The chorus gathers around a chanting refrain of 'we were here!', later reprised in the album's final track and as the title of a book documenting the album's creation and tour. In three simple words, Tuomas recognises the miraculous fact that we were able to exist at all, a topic Dawkins would return to in *The Greatest Show on Earth*, but the singalong peak also acts as a collective unifier. Whether a connecting tie for a thousand-strong audience at a Nightwish show or a humble reminder of the journey we are sharing right this moment with the billions of others alive today, there is an undeniable energy seeping from 'Alpenglow' and at its heart is a touching togetherness.

Its wise placing towards the end of the tracklist helps amplify its message of reflection and accomplishment. There's a hark back to 'My Walden', again reinterpreted under the lens of community as Floor sings of 'building a Walden of our own'. When the lyrics later become a direct address, the song moulds into a one-to-one conversation with every single listener: 'you are my path, my home my star'; less of a romance, more of a familial unity.

Sometimes, however, the message of presence had to be reinforced. During one show, frustrated with a disengaging ocean of cameras, Tuomas commented in *We Were Here* of Floor's introduction of the song:

> She introduced 'Alpenglow' something like this: 'This song is about love and living in the moment, so stuff your fuckin' phones in your pockets and enjoy the show!' And it actually worked – people obeyed her.

The seeds for the digital takedown of *Human. :||: Nature.*'s 'Noise' had been sown.

'Alpenglow' was Nuclear Blast's choice as first single, and whilst it would have been a safer option than the two that were chosen, it eventually received the equally rewarding status of fan favourite. Tuomas himself even remarked in early promotions that the song was, in many ways, the ultimate Nightwish song. Immortalised on both the Wembley and Tampere shows recorded for *Vehicle of Spirit*, the rapturous response from audiences could well convince a casual Nightwish attendee that the song was up there with their biggest hit singles.

'The Eyes of Sharbat Gula' 6:03 (Music: Tuomas Holopainen)

Whilst not intricately weaved within the core concept, the record's reverence of the miracle of life gives further weight to the difficult and harsh realities of which 'The Eyes of Sharbat Gula' draws its inspiration. The instrumental track was initially intended to tell the story of children in war, its title lifted from the internationally recognised image that adorned *National Geographic*. The photograph taken by Steve McCurry was titled *Afghan Girl* – the name of the girl, Sharbat Gula, later discovered following the global interest in the picture. With striking untamed eyes in McCurry's original, the picture was recreated in the *Endless Forms Most Beautiful* booklet by long-term collaborator ToxicAngel. This time, the Afghan girl closes her eyes, a small mercy asserting that children should never bear witness to such violence.

It's Troy Donockley that we hear first, delivering pained expressions reflecting on the song's inspiration, mournful and grieving. When the children's choir eventually enter around the song's midpoint there's a sense of naivete and innocence retained to their voices; a striking juxtaposition to the violent surroundings from which they emerge. The decision to keep the track as an instrumental was born of Troy's suggestion and Tuomas' own difficulties, as he told German site EMP:

> I was really struggling with the lyrics, I wrote pages and pages of lyrics and just didn't feel right at all because the subject is so delicate. It's so important. How do I nail this? And then, when Troy heard the original demo that I had,

> he said this is beautiful and hypnotic but it doesn't need any lyrics. It's much more powerful if it only has some distant voices, maybe a children's choir etc. And that was a revelation to me, that's exactly how it should be done because now it gives food for imagination.

'The Greatest Show on Earth' (i. 'Four Point Six', ii. 'Life', iii. 'The Toolmaker', iv. 'The Understanding', v. 'Sea-Worn Driftwood') 24:00 (Music: Tuomas Holopainen, Marco Hietala ('The Toolmaker'), lyrics: Tuomas Holopainen)

If the title wasn't fanfare enough, Tuomas remarked in a track-by-track with *Spazio Rock* that 'The Greatest Show on Earth' is the main act of the album'. It's not to discredit any of the other songs on the tracklist to say that this sprawling epic has clearly had, as it needed, the most attention and focus on its composition. Its lyrical message core to '*Endless Forms Most Beautiful*', its galvanising refrain launched already in 'Alpenglow' and the voice of Richard Dawkins teased at the very opening of the album – Tuomas was right, it had all been building to this.

Recognising the song as the album's centrepiece, it very nearly became the title of the album, betraying the humble nature of the band's songwriter. This, and a desire for something a little more unusual, resulted in Darwin's quote *Endless Forms Most Beautiful* being chosen for the album instead. It felt a fair compromise, still acknowledging the prominent evolutionary muse, unlike the other leading title suggestions of *Élan* and the self-titled *Nightwish*.

If any topic needed a weighty twenty-four-minute runtime, it's the miraculous chronicle of evolution. Spanning 4.6 billion years, the song accelerates from the big bang to the emergence of life from single-celled organisms through to the Anthropocene present. It dares to gaze into the future too, envisaging the end of days for humankind and what might happen to the earth after our disappearance, expressed in sparse whale song. Spoiler alert – it's pretty content without us.

In *We Were Here*, Tuomas recounted the creative freedom when it came to translating creation and destruction into sound:

> I had endless possibilities in my hands for 'The Greatest Show on Earth'. What is the sound of crumpling continental plates that mountains are made of? Or the disintegration of radioactive components? Or the sound of space particles bombarding the earth? And how would I refer to immortal works of music composed by man? Well, I included shades of 'Dies Irae' by Thomas Celano, 'Toccata' and 'Fuga' by Johann Sebastian Bach, banjo music from Western movies, 'Rock around the Clock' by Bill Haley & His Comets, and 'Enter Sandman' by Metallica. I was also thinking about borrowing 'Sandstorm' by Darude, but in the end, we just went for an unrecognisable techno loop.

These musical interpolations are brief moments in which the expansive track aligns with the present day from which it was composed. The sounds are interweaved into the track's ultimate crescendo towards the end of the section 'The Toolmaker'; composed alongside Marco Hietala, it warns of 'self-destructive weaponry' and 'giant mushroom clouds' at such a rapid, driving pace that an escape from destruction feels too fleeting to imagine. The invigorating, sing-along summit of 'we were here!' announces the end of mankind – it is dominant and fearful, anguished and powerful. From there, the song descends from explosive eruptions to a humble, pure piano melody. The moment of reflection asks the listener to sit with these feelings of loss and disaster for a moment ('The Understanding') before Richard Dawkins delivers his longest and most impactful quote of the album – a reading from his book *Unweaving the Rainbow: Science, Delusion and the Appetite for Wonder* – the biologist bringing forth a comforting, stirring reminder of the miracle of life, forcing the gaze away from death and back towards life.

Naturally, the band's lengthiest composition to date garnered plenty of interest from the off, but the most intriguing aspect of *Endless Forms Most Beautiful* was the inclusion of Dawkins. It was arguably a risky move, too, with Dawkins often demonised by religious groups for his writing, most profoundly on the release of his million-selling book *The God Delusion*. This wasn't lost on Troy and Tuomas, self-confessed Dawkins fanatics, as Troy recalled to *Metal Blast*:

> If what we had was [Richard Dawkins] saying beautiful, universal things, statements of universal beauty and love, you couldn't criticise them. It wasn't explicit atheism; it was humanism, universalism… Jukka, Tuomas and I, [were] sitting in a hotel room in New Zealand, with a bottle of fine shiraz wine, talking about the book *The Magic of Reality*, by Richard Dawkins (as well as *The God Delusion* and *The Selfish Gene)*. We watched a couple of his lectures, and I stupidly, after we had drank a few glasses of wine, said that it would be wonderful to have him in the new album, and decided to promise that I would find him and get him. Of course, I woke up the next morning wondering, 'what have I done?! What have I said!?'

Dawkins admitted to not being aware of Nightwish, much fonder of classical composers than European metal acts. In an interview with *Prog* magazine, the message of the album and Dawkins' own beliefs had clearly aligned remarkably, Dawkins stating:

> Science should be an inspiration to musicians – it is a positive thing. I have always emphasised the importance of the poetic approach to science. What we should be celebrating is the poetry within reality.

Not content with committing Dawkins to record and exposing him to international metal audiences, the group also asked him to join them for their momentous Wembley show, a proud expression all round as Dawkins received an ecstatic response from the audience.

Dawkins was only a part of the vast symphony, over 600 individual elements eventually finalised for what promised to be Nightwish's latest masterpiece. Upon the album's release, 'The Greatest Show on Earth' was met with an immediate acclaim from both critics and listeners alike. It soon became another setlist mainstay, not an easy task for a time-devouring epic, shaving off only a few minutes of its runtime. Live, the band acknowledged the natural peak of 'The Toolmaker', taking their bows during Dawkins' spoken word and fading to black shortly before the whale song of the studio cut. Short of inviting the said whales to perform live onstage, it's hard to imagine just how the ambition of 'The Greatest Show on Earth' can ever be surpassed.

'Sagan' 4:45 (Music and lyrics: Tuomas Holopainen)

Any loyalists disappointed with the single choice of 'Élan' were fruitfully rewarded with the pure, concise, and familiar Nightwish sound of 'Sagan'. Much more in line with the likes of 'Storytime' and 'Amaranth', it became another B-side that fans pondered long and hard on why it had been omitted. Tuomas answered that very question in *We Were Here*, stating that: 'lyrically 'Sagan' would have suited the themes better, and it was originally meant to be on the album instead of 'Yours is an Empty Hope', but in the end, we felt that the album needed a heavier track, so 'Sagan' ended up as the second track on the 'Élan' single. Speaking to *LoudTV*, Tuomas also confirmed that plans to make the album a twelve-track opus were stunted by CD runtime limitations.

Carl Sagan completes the trilogy of inspirations for the album and whilst Dawkins can be heard reciting both his and Darwin's words on the record, he also lent his voice to a trio of Sagan's quotes, some of which were instead printed in the album's booklet. Two of these very quotes are idyllic bridges from the themes of *Imaginaerum* and the evolutionary scope of its follow-up, Sagan remarking that 'Imagination will often carry us to worlds that never were, but without it, we go nowhere'. Self-confessed Dawkins fanboy Tuomas has insisted that the unused recordings from the writer have been kept for prosperity and may well make an appearance in future live shows.

The idea of imagination as a crucial driver is echoed in the lyrics of 'Sagan', the snappiest line closing out the chorus: 'woe to all who stop at the horizon'. The song's tribute to 'sending all the poets to the stars' would also lean forward to the band's next album, with songs such as 'Shoemaker' and 'Ad Astra' both retaining that curious gaze deep into the night sky. The latter would also feature an extended quote from Carl Sagan and his book *Pale Blue Dot*.

Nightwish Cruise Live Covers (Various)

Onboard the Nightwish cruise (yes, really!), a show like none other was unfolding. Whilst the band's live approach was geared toward grand spectacles, the limitations of a cruise ship were a suitable opportunity to draw back on the budget without sacrificing the element of surprise. Giving founding members Tuomas and Emppu the night off, the performances began with Troy and Marco's acoustic takes on Pink Floyd's 'Money', 'Wonderful Life' by English singer Black, 'Locomotive Breath' by Jethro Tull and sing-a-long favourite 'Rock around the Clock' from Bill Haley & His Comets. The latter of which proved a nice tie-in for the *Endless Forms Most Beautiful* touring cycle as it was very briefly sampled in 'The Greatest Show on Earth'.

A cover of 'Ace of Spades' just didn't feel correct without a percussive foundation and thus, Kai was welcomed into the fold before Floor joined the trio for a winning finale of Heart's 'Alone' (a number she had also covered with After Forever), a debut live performance of 'Edema Ruh' in a stripped back styling and a rehash of 'The Mug of Brown Ale' which had peppered setlists since *Imaginaerum*.

Finally, the campfire acoustics of Nightwish were fully realised, albeit without the mastermind himself on the stage. Instead, for the first time in his life, Holopainen was able to sit back with a beer and enjoy the band he had tirelessly dedicated himself to, all whilst sailing the Baltic Sea.

'Elvenjig' 2:50 (Music: Iona)

Something old, something new. When 'Elvenpath' was chosen for inclusion on the *Decades* tour setlist, it was preceded each night by a folky instrumental segue titled 'Elvenjig', a shorter and heavier take on the song 'Jigs' by Troy Donockley's former band Iona. It crams a lot into its short runtime, capturing the boisterous nature of *Oceanborn*'s 'Moondance' before the keyboards give way to Troy's leading pipes, a knowing nod to Nightwish's ever-growing folk influence.

Human. :||: Nature. (2020)

Personnel:
Floor Jansen: vocals
Troy Donockley: uilleann pipes, low whistles, bouzouki, bodhran, aerophone, space guitars, vocals
Tuomas Holopainen: keys
Emppu Vuorinen: guitars
Marko Hietala: bass, vocals, acoustic guitar
Kai Hahto: drums, percussion
London Philharmonic (credited as Pale Blue Orchestra): orchestra
Jenny O'Grady: choirmaster
Metro Voices: choir
Richard Ihnatowicz: music preparation
James Shearman: orchestra and choir conductor, orchestration and arrangement ('How's the Heart', 'Procession')
Martin Higgins: assistant orchestration and arrangement ('How's The Heart', 'Procession')
Mat Bartram: orchestra engineer
Laura Beck: orchestra engineer assistant
Pip Williams: arranger, orchestrator and director ('Music', 'Noise', 'Shoemaker', 'Harvest', 'Pan', 'Tribal', 'Endlessness', 'All The Works of Nature Which Adorn the World')
Geraldine James: spoken word ('Vista', 'Ad Astra')
Johanna Kurkela: spoken word ('Shoemaker')
Recorded and engineered by Tero Kinnunen, Mikko Karmila and Troy Donockley at Petrax Studio, Troykington Castle, Angel Studios, Finnvox Studios and Röskö Campsite
Recorded between August and October 2019
Arranged by Tuomas Holopainen, Marko Hietala, Emppu Vuorinen, Floor Jansen, Kai Hahto, Troy Donockley, Tero Kinnunen
Mixed by Mikko Karmila at Finnvox Studios between October and December 2019
Produced by Tuomas Holopainen
Mika Jussila: mastering
ToxicAngel and Ravnheart: artwork and layout
Tim Tronckoe: photography
Tim Martindale: photography
Andrea Beckers: photography
Tina Korhonen: photography
Mikko Tirkkonen: additional photography
Mikko Nevalainen: additional photography
Kari Pennanen: additional photography
Burt Farner: additional photography
Steve MacIntyre: additional photography
Jani Havunen: additional photography

Whilst fans certainly hadn't been starved in the duration thanks to the *Decades* tour, when *Human. :||: Nature.* was announced, it was to close the longest gap between Nightwish albums in their history. At this stage in their career, curious mumblings were like a broken record as audiences wondered *yet again* how Tuomas could topple his own peak following the veneration reserved for 'The Greatest Show on Earth'. The answer? An entire disc dedicated to the vastness of nature, almost entirely instrumental and not a riff in sight.

Whilst it may not have been the band's most adored venture, the ambition was astounding. Not only was 'All the Works of Nature Which Adorn the World' a compositional labyrinth, tacking it onto the end of a metal record put a refreshing amount of trust in listeners. Admittedly, Nightwish have often existed on the peripheries of heavy metal, but a full orchestral detour was still something of a creative risk.

Endless Forms Most Beautiful was often touted as an album of two halves, 'The Greatest Show on Earth' and, well... the rest. *Human. :||:. Nature* took this concept even further, putting a physical stopgap between the two sides of the album – unless, of course, listeners are experiencing the record via streaming. The two sides can also stand alone; the first disc feels complete in its journey from the ambient opening of 'Music' to the grand, doomy closer 'Endlessness' whilst the suite of orchestral tracks is naturally within its own sphere. Then we have the punctuative nightmare of the album title, using pipes or the musical 'repeat sign' (:||:) to separate or unite, depending on your reading, both of the album's muses: humankind and the natural world.

Never before had Tuomas seemed less concerned with commercial success as evidenced by a significant lack of clear singles on offer. 'Noise' served as the album's lead despite pushing an almost six-minute length, and though 'How's the Heart?' offered a more straightforward structure, the rest of the songs glisten in their unpredictability. Perhaps reinforcing the more experimental nature of the album, 'Harvest' was a divisive choice for second single. As many pined for Floor, they got Troy on lead vocals and whilst yearning for bombast, they received a folky singalong midtempo. In hindsight, it was a necessary reset of expectations when approaching the proggier stylings of the album.

If *Endless Forms Most Beautiful* paid tribute to the earth, *Human. :||: Nature.* cast a gaze towards the stars. 'Shoemaker' honoured the late American geologist whose ashes were sent to the moon, whilst 'Ad Astra' (translated as 'To the Stars') is the soaring finale of disc two. Despite its place as said conclusion on the disc of instrumental songs, 'Ad Astra' was chosen as a pre-release track to announce Nightwish's partnership with the World Land Trust and later became the only 'chapter' of the suite to be included in a live set.

As the group geared up to tour the album, the Covid-19 pandemic struck and cast all touring plans into disarray. The usual routine of write, record, release, tour was disrupted and had significant repercussions for Marco

Hietala. Disenfranchised with the industry, Hietala handed in his resignation before any of the supporting tour dates for the album had taken place. Citing his reasons in a press release, he commented:

> For quite a few years now, I haven't been able to feel validated by this life. We have streaming company big guns demanding 9/5 work from artists of inspiration while unfairly sharing the profits. Even among the artists. We're the banana republic of the music industry. Biggest tour promoters squeeze percentages even from our own merchandise while paying dividends to Middle East. Apparently, some theocrasies can take the money from the music that would get you beheaded or jailed there without appearing as hypocrites. Just a couple of examples here. This past year forced me to stay home and think. And I found myself very disillusioned about these and a lot of things. I found out that I am in need of that validation. For me to write, sing and play, I need to find some new reasons and inspirations. 'My Walden' so to speak

Unlike Jukka's continued insomnia struggles and Anette and Tarja's growing tensions, the split took the rest of the band by surprise. Once again, Tuomas felt that Nightwish's future was in jeopardy, believing that Hietala's departure may well have meant the end of the band. He soon reconsidered and worked with the rest of the group towards a pair of virtual shows, *An Evening with Nightwish in a Virtual World*. Whilst the shows were postponed following Hietala's announcement, they served as a fitting welcome for Wintersun's Jukka Koskinen as his temporary replacement to see out the *Human. :||: Nature.* tour and the two virtual events. Passing his unofficial probation, Koskinen would later be confirmed as Hietala's permanent replacement midway through the album's tour cycle.

After numerous pandemic-imposed delays, the *Human. :||: Nature.* tour finally began in earnest in 2022. For the first time since the band's early days, the tour coincides with the work on the group's upcoming tenth studio record and, whilst other artists may be tempted to slip in a few new songs to test the waters, the notoriously secretive Holopainen will likely keep his burgeoning compositions to himself. Until then, the album's long-awaited chance to bask in the spotlight will tide fans over, galvanised by a solitary few years of isolation and separation, although what better time to heed the call of the band's work and take a walk in the woods, gaze at the stars and appreciate the everyday, pondering what humble magic will inspire Tuomas next.

'Music' 7:23 (Music and lyrics: Tuomas Holopainen)

A song about music could easily swerve into pretentious territory and with *Human. :||: Nature.*'s tracklist also teasing a later interpolation of the oldest piece of annotated music in existence, it would be fair to proceed with caution. Indeed, a progressive trip through genres had been floated, as Tuomas discussed with *Metal Hammer* UK:

> I wanted to write a song about music. What is music? It's such an interesting philosophical question. At some point, I had this really pretentious idea of doing the first riff metal, then jazz and punk. I tried it and it sounded awful. The worst thing ever.

Rather than showing off an expansive knowledge of musical history, though, 'Music' is more of an evangelical praising of this newly discovered sorcery. It asks you to imagine being the very first person to discover melodies, the power of sound, the swell of a song and hails the ability of music to help us relate ('singing the tale of another man'), remain present ('deepening the listening') and delve into escapism ('losing yourself to the endless symphony').

Immediately the album continues where 'The Greatest Show on Earth' left off, emerging from the oceanic soundscape that closed out *Endless Forms Most Beautiful*. 'Thematically we're sailing the same waters, ' Tuomas told *FaceCulture*, and in many ways 'Music' tackles a similarly enormous scope as the closing epic – this time following the journey of music from the harmonious hum of creatures and nature aligning to the curious, tentative discovery (and eventual exploitation) by mankind. With a sparse arrangement and a timid flutter from Jansen, the group approach their muse with quiet, considered steps before the second chorus surges to an elated refrain – all the liberation and joy of blissful music underpinning the sonic peak.

A proggier steer is apparent from the off as 'Music' doesn't venture into its first verse for over three minutes, instead swimming towards an expanding drone sound, surfacing for a tribal percussive march, and then submerging again for a bubbling, dissonant piano. As we wash up on shore, a moody goosebump-inducing melody welcomes us to the song proper – an entire journey undertaken before Jansen has uttered a single word.

As is tradition with Tuomas' writing, a healthy dose of realism is also present – berating greedy crowds and demanding audiences as our humble discovery of music becomes a capitalist tool. The twist in the tale could be read as a comment on the underhand music business or a response to those critical of the long periods between Nightwish records in recent years. It also tied in with a defiant stance that Jansen has upheld regarding personal boundaries and the sometimes excessive expectations of fans.

'Noise' 5:41 (Music and lyrics: Tuomas Holopainen)

From music emerges 'Noise', a takedown of distracted blindness caused by screen obsessions. The message is loud, clear, and relatable, telling of a civilisation marching with heads down and gaze fixed on endlessly refreshing social media channels. One of the few titbits Tuomas offered during the writing sessions for the album was that Charlie Brooker and Annabel Jones' Netflix series *Black Mirror* was an inspiration, and on 'Noise', the show even gets a direct reference in one lyric: 'feast your eyes on the black mirror'. As with the show, the song is a warning against an overreliance on technology that could steadily begin to take over our lives, but Tuomas insisted to *GoetiaMedia* that the message was also a hopeful one:

> Me, all the bandmembers, we love technology. We wouldn't ever have done this record without technology. We love our cell phones, the Internet and all that, but it's a criticism for the addiction that these things cause in human beings. 'Addiction' is the word. It's such a shame that we have all these wonderful tools that we can for the good, to spread true information and to be connected to the world. I love the idea of social media, I like Twitter, that everybody in the world suddenly has a voice; we have a voice... It's just a matter of what you put out there.

Upon its release, *Human. :||: Nature.* was forced to adapt to yet more online trends. Every single song was immediately launched with its own lyric video, providing a visual element and, had it been up to Tuomas, that's where it would have ended. The costly task of making an official promotional clip was an expense that the bandleader felt unnecessary. He wasn't alone either, Iron Maiden instead commissioned animated clips for their recently released *Senjutsu* album and power metal icons Rhapsody of Fire hedging their bets on lyric videos for two of their three 2019 releases. It was Floor that eventually convinced Tuomas of the promotional power of a video, proven correct by the clip surpassing the album's lyric videos by some 5 million views.

Although the song didn't need a visual companion to clarify its message, the directorial work of *Imaginaerum* movie collaborator Stobe Harju made 'Noise' one of Nightwish's finest visual feasts to date. The band's outfits looked refined and dystopian, crowning Troy as a king, and turning Jansen's floor-length gown into a cage. The most memorable scene sees an audience sitting before the Mona Lisa, the entirety fixated on their phones instead of the world-famous artwork before them. Leave it to the mischievous Emppu to break away from the crowd, punished for his disobedience as a 'slave of the brave new world'. It isn't all doom and gloom, though; the end of the video pans to a mesmerising sunrise, offering that an escape from the artificial numbness is within reach.

'Shoemaker' 5:20 (Music and lyrics: Tuomas Holopainen)

'Shoemaker' is the song that fans had been longing for since Floor Jansen's introduction as the band's vocalist. Keenly aware of her powerful operatic skills that had been demonstrated throughout her work with After Forever, it finally culminated in the satisfying, soaring ode which transports the listener to the stars, alongside the touching story of its muse.

It tells the story of the titular Eugene Shoemaker, the American geologist that discovered the comet Shoemaker-Levy during a lifetime of dedication to planetary science. Following his untimely death after a car accident in 1997, some of his ashes were sent to the moon two years later to honour his work and legacy. The song's lyrics celebrate his final resting place with Holopainen's usual poetic flair: 'Now you've been tucked in for eternal earthrise and wonder... yours is the whole starmap of heavens, of myriad endings'.

It's remarkable that it took so long for Tuomas' wife and Auri collaborator Johanna Kurkela to appear on a Nightwish record, if not counting her uncredited contribution amongst countless others to *Imaginaerum*'s 'Song of Myself'. Her gentle recitation tackles the *Romeo and Juliet* quote that was included on Eugene Shoemaker's memorial capsule before the music withdraws as if lifted from earth and into the atmosphere. Floor's vocalisations serenade Shoemaker's final journey, ever more grand and soaring as the song reaches its climax. You'd be forgiven for thinking that these vocal gymnastics are second nature to Jansen, so effortless is her delivery, but she told *Distorted Sound* of the difficulty that arose when tackling the striking finale of the song:

> The end of Shoemaker, where there's this operatic part, I needed to get it exactly right – not too big, not too little, not too light, not too Maria Callas. What I learned mostly is that you need so much patience with things you haven't written yourself. I wanted to get everything at once, but it's way too complex, you have to dissect it basically into manageable parts: first the melody, then the words, then the phrasing. You have to develop muscle memory for it, then there's fine-tuning, and then there's learning what the lyrics are about! I can't do everything at once. I've learnt to be more patient. Allow things to not be good for a while, because it takes time. Eventually, you want complex things to sound easy. The message and the feeling is the most important part. For instance, the end of 'Shoemaker', we finished recording it, heard it back, and tried again. Once everything was put together, it still didn't feel quite right, we all felt it. At home, I got a fantastic microphone, sang it, and it just worked! It's a very meticulous process.

'Harvest' 5:13 (Music and lyrics: Tuomas Holopainen)
'Harvest' was a curious choice for second single; whilst 'Noise' was just enough of the Nightwish sound to appease ravenous fans, the sophomore release reset expectations for the album and assured that there would be plenty of musical curveballs to anticipate. It isn't that listeners weren't already well-versed in the band's folkish leanings, but 'Harvest' felt like the closest the band had ever come to a Disney ballad, somewhere between 'Circle of Life' from *The Lion King* and *Aladdin*'s 'A Whole New World'.

Thankfully, there are enough elements to prevent it becoming too cloying. The lyrics are a stark contrast to the cheerful melody, Tuomas describing it as 'a song laughing at death… smiling at the scythe'. 'Harvest' celebrates that march towards death but casts aside fear, instead revering the union of our shared fates and heeding the lessons of acceptance and appreciation shared by Richard Dawkins on the album prior. The structure of the song is also far more adventurous than a usual single, creeping out from a persistent drumbeat and eerie vocal lines that establish the initial curiosity and inherent trepidation of pondering your own eventual demise. Fear not, it doesn't linger for too long – inviting in an excitable, dance-break as if soundtracking the contagious cheer of a maypole dance.

Whilst the entirety of *Human. :||: Nature.* was penned by Holopainen alone, 'Harvest' is indisputably Troy's song. Naturally, his pipes are prominent in the up-tempo middle section but it's his voice front and centre that proved to be the biggest talking point. It's another place where Nightwish have opted to circumvent maximalist expectations, Troy's humble and soft voice worlds away from Tarja and Floor's operatic heights. The more versatile vocal approach of the album was borne from the *Decades* tour, in which harmonies played a significant role in reimagining some of their older work. Underlining Donockley's inimitable presence on the track, Tuomas told *FaceCulture*: 'Harvest' was tailor-made for Troy to sing, it has a strong Irish vibe in it, you're in the moors… it was just a natural thing to keep it for Troy'.

'Pan' 5:18 (Music and lyrics: Tuomas Holopainen)

My, how things have changed since the *Imaginaerum* days. *Endless Forms Most Beautiful* firmly planted the band in reality, prioritising science over storybooks and it may have seemed that *Human. :||: Nature.* was keenly following suit. 'Pan' makes it clear that imagination and the vitality of creation that inspired the band's 2012 record is still a topic worthy of reverence and recognition. Tuomas told *Metal Hammer* UK:

> Pan is an ode to human imagination. One of my biggest literary heroes, Neil Gaiman, said it the best: 'Fairy tales are more than true: not because they tell us that dragons exist, but because they tell us that dragons can be beaten'.

The lyrics could have been lifted directly from the Olzon years, reading as a mix of 'Escapist', and 'Storytime', singing of a 'pale blue theatre stage' (a stage for an ocean soul?), 'sleeping stories unimagined' and a neat segue between imagination and evolution in 'an ape in awe before a door to labyrinth'. It isn't difficult to see why 'Pan' resonated with fans on first listen, particularly those longing for a return to the imaginative concerns of years before.

Leaving the orchestral elements to the second disc of the album, it's startling to consider that the first side of *Human. :||: Nature.* made do with only strings and choirs. That realisation is never more striking than on 'Pan', which sits amongst the group's most bombastic anthems in recent years, highlighting the choral elements in the descending, playful middle eight. Although 'Pan' felt like a vibrant shoo-in for the live set, the song was given its sole live performance during the group's virtual shows. Surely a live set inclusion remains on the horizon?

'How's the Heart?' 5:02 (Music and lyrics: Tuomas Holopainen)
If 'My Walden' was a continuation of 'I Want My Tears Back', 'How's the Heart?' completes the trinity of sing-along folk-led numbers. As Troy's pipes break through the riffs, it's somewhat comforting to be in familiar territory once more. It could also be argued that the track is the most instant and accessible cut from the record and would have served well as a single, eventually receiving a promotional release when 500 vinyl copies were issued by Finnish record store Lipposen Levy Ja Kasetti. It was no surprise either when Troy and Floor dug out the song in an acoustic rendition during the album's promo tour as a captivating invitation into what the album had to offer.

In the band's countdown to the album's release, Tuomas described the song as:

> Human empathy, altruism, true love. They truly are the better angels of our nature. The nature of the humankind. We have the potential to be such a great species, and in many ways, we already are. It is really important to remember to ask your family, your friends, strangers, and yourself the question: How's The Heart?

'How's the Heart?' is the logical next stop for those heeding the warning of 'Noise'. It preaches connection and presence, challenging us to turn away from the virtual world and instead towards the time-worn ask of 'how are you?'. The title may sound a little clumsy, but the message of the song is knowing and astute; 'How's the Heart' underlines just how important that very question can be, something that is asked countless times each day whilst never expecting an honest answer. Understandably, the song stood out following *Human. :||: Nature.*'s mid-pandemic release; amongst the madness, it found an audience that were learning to appreciate the earnestness of its message.

'Procession' 5:31 (Music and lyrics: Tuomas Holopainen)
Having given us a dose of bombast and a folky romp, the band indulge themselves with the most unusual track on disc one. 'Procession' boasts ten verses and no chorus to speak of, Tuomas describing it to *Metal Hammer* UK as 'a relentless build-up'. The zenith that it edges towards is a lyrical twist, reframing the entire reading of the lyrics – 'Procession' was Nightwish taking their most confident steer from the prog world to date.

The message seems familiar at first as Floor traverses through centuries, the last lyric of each verse welcoming acorns, heartbeats, suffering, writing and wisdom. As the song reaches its climax, the narrator is revealed and – spoiler alert – it's our evolutionary descendants. Unfortunately, just as on the last album, the end of humanity doesn't sound like much fun: 'we will remember all the suffering… we were there and will remember mankind'. It's a haunting realisation as our own obituary is sung to us, a dark surprise as the song swells to its finale.

'Procession' is highly likely to remain a studio experiment, Floor commenting to *Distorted Sound* that 'some songs are just not good live songs, like 'Procession' would never really work'. Still, its role in the album is profound, underlining the human theme of the first disc by detailing mankind's end, though in the compositional respect, it served as a comparative launchpad for Tuomas, who commented:

> 'Procession' was the starting point for the whole songwriting process for *Human. :||: Nature.*, it was the first song to get its final form and I remember vividly looking at the first season of the series *Stranger Things* and was heavily inspired by the soundscapes and arpeggios of the soundtrack…. that's how the song got started. It's very lyric-heavy … you need to delve into the lyrics and also, personally, I feel that this is the best, most touching performance by Floor that I've ever heard. She really captures the essence of the song and tells the story as it should be told.

'Tribal' 3:56 (Music and lyrics: Tuomas Holopainen)

If 'Harvest' belonged to Troy, 'Tribal' was a dedicated showcase for Kai Hahto on his first album as an official Nightwish member. The drumming in the song is some of the most prominent in Nightwish's entire catalogue and Kai took his responsibility very seriously, revealing in the album countdown:

> When I heard it for the first time as a demo, I had this vision in my head that I can't really play the stuff I want to play with my old drumkit, so I had to come up with the new setup and I actually added five more drums on my left side to be able to play some of the stuff on the album. 'Tribal' is one of the best examples… it's really percussive'.

Percussive is the right word, echoing the song's theme of tribal mindsets and herd mentality. It's right that the song sounds harsh and intimidating, a scorned cult making cruel demands long after the alluring warmth of belonging has subsided. It'd be naïve to say that such communities don't still exist today, but 'Tribal' casts the band back to myriad years ago as Tuomas told *FaceCulture*:

> When the idea of doing a song about tribalism [came up], about cults, about why we want so desperately to belong to a certain tribe... I thought OK,

> this is the theme, how do we execute this? So then we thought, how would a band sound like twenty thousand years ago if you gave them modern technology? Naturally, it would be very percussive, very primitive, very tribal, really heavy, dissonant and that's how the song ended up being...

The primitive nature reveals itself as the song descends into grunts during its mid-section before a crushing drum solo spirals the song to its catastrophic close. In keeping with its intent of sounding like an early pack of humans were at the helm, 'Tribal' cares little about refrains in its second half and instead seems to wander in numerous directions at its own discretion, first drawing back to sparsity before building to a frantic pace. In the last seconds of bedlam, each instrument forges forward as if trying to outrun one another, a violent hunt in amongst the havoc.

'Endlessness' 7:10 (Music and lyrics: Tuomas Holopainen)
Serendipitously apt, the final song from the disc features Marco Hietala front and centre on his swan song contribution to the Nightwish catalogue. By the time 'Endlessness' rolls around, over forty minutes into the record, Hietala's voice has been noticeably scant save for a few harmony contributions; the penetrating closer rewards the wait as a doomy influence twists the band in yet another unexpected direction, and who better to serenade this esoteric farewell?

It wasn't a case of each member being handed a vocal 'solo' arbitrarily for the first disc – instead, the voice was a significant consideration to underline the human side of the double disc as Tuomas told Carl Begai at *BraveWords*:

> We wanted to focus on the vocal performances. It's the human part of the album, you need to hear the human voice. There are a lot of lyrics, there is a lot going on, but that was a deliberate decision: let's get everything that we have out of these vocalists.

Whilst Floor contributes to the middle eight, it's a wise choice to give Marco the bulk of the track, allowing him to transcend the full journey from the yearning of the refrain ('someone in the tomorrow is waiting for me') to the dulcifying closing verses that wind down with a sense of contentment as a guitar wails into the ether. Many may consider it too sombre of a farewell for the charismatic jester, but Marco's exit will forever be tied with 'Endlessness', a stirring exit from one of the band's most popular members.

In light of Marco's departure, Tuomas shared that the song would not be considered for inclusion on the virtual shows of 2021 and has remained unplayed during the *Human. :||: Nature.* tour. Regardless of its missing vocalist, 'Endlessness' also remains an outlier in Nightwish's discography for its doom influence, harking back to Tuomas' influences of My Dying Bride and gothic purveyors Tiamat. The track isn't entirely built on the bleak misery that the doom genre is known for, but that element of dread is a necessary underscore to the resonance of the tranquil ending – a brave, nervous venture into the endless dark.

'All The Works of Nature Which Adorn the World' 30:58 ('Vista', 'The Blue', 'The Green', 'Moors', 'Aurorae', 'Quiet as the Snow', 'Anthropocene (inc. Hurrian Hymn to Nikkal)', 'Ad Astra') (Music and lyrics: Tuomas Holopainen)

Any listener missing the broad soundscapes on the first disc need only flip to the second side of *Human. :||: Nature.* – a solely orchestral suite spanning half an hour and comprising almost entirely of instrumental arrangements. If the progressive leanings on the first disc suggested an intent to push the boundaries, the mere existence of this expansive composition throws a roguish grin towards metal traditionalists.

With every Nightwish album appearing to widen the scope of possibility, it wouldn't be unwise to assume that 'All the Works of Nature Which Adorn the World' was yet another attempt to exceed expectations. In contrast, however, Troy shared with Carl Begai at *BraveWords* that the piece originated solely as a passion project for the band's own enjoyment:

> The second disc wasn't designed for anybody else; it was designed to entertain us. If other people get some enrichment from it in whatever way, imaginatively or sonically, that's an added bonus. It could be seen as a really brilliant move for Nightwish, but we can't anticipate how people are going to react. It could be seen as adventurous, as a folly, but you really can't consider such things when you're writing music.

The linguistic contributions of the track are drawn from a diverse array of influences. The song's title is lifted from an entry in Leonardo DaVinci's notebook, whilst the piece commences with a recitation from Byron's *Childe Harold's Pilgrimage* – consciously ending with the poignant admission 'I love not man less, but nature more'. Following the vocal contribution of English actress Geraldine James, it's nature and not man that retakes central focus. A percussive, tumultuous sea beckons in 'The Blue', serene strings and piano look out onto the vastness of 'The Green', and those familiar Nightwish pipes are a warm companion in the windy moors.

The bombast of Nightwish's usual sound is most present on 'Aurorae' as the shimmering phenomenon echoes the band's mission statement – the awe-inspiring magic of reality. Tuomas appeased nervous fans ahead of the song's release, telling *Metal Hammer* UK:

> When you listen to the song, it's very Nightwish. The essence of it, the melodies, the overall feel... it's basically Nightwish's love letter to planet earth.

> We love the beauty of this planet. Starting from the seas to the meadows, the northern lights, the snowy landscapes and off to the stars we go.

Glistening bells and a rare vocal contribution present 'Quiet as the Snow'; the layered murmurs of Floor Jansen repeat the title phrase in numerous languages. It's an interesting technique, the voice easily blending in with the broad instruments contributing to the constantly remoulding atmospheres. Tense strings transition into the Anthropocene epoch in which humanity's destruction looms on the horizon, though the band instead choose to highlight the oldest notated song in the world, 'Hurrian Hymn to Nikkal', a nice nod back to the first disc in which the discovery of music is retold in *Human. :||: Nature*'s opening track.

With landscapes, oceans and phenomena traversed, the song reaches its immense finale by soaring into the atmosphere. 'Ad Astra' not only ascends above the earth, it also became the suite's only extraction to make it into the live set and to a promo single release, amplified into Nightwish territory by Floor's vocalisations which serenade the dazzling flight. As the song forges forth into the heavens, it anchors itself by recalling the touching story of 'Shoemaker' and incorporating an extended quote from *Endless Forms Most Beautiful* muse Carl Sagan – his piece *Pale Blue Dot* marvelling at the enormity of the world and our small place in it. As the immense time-travelling, stargazing trip draws to an end, the thought-provoking Sagan quote resonates: 'That's here. That's home. That's us'.

Compilations

Wishmastour 2000 (2000)

The French compilation with the punny title, *Wishmastour 2000,* was essentially an extended single of the parent album's title track. Alongside 'Wishmaster', a handful of B-sides and rarities were included as well as enhanced videos for 'Sleeping Sun' and a live performance of 'Sacrament of Wilderness'. *Wishmastour 2000* is far from essential for anyone other than determined collectors but technically scored a plaudit as the first of many compilations released under the Nightwish name.

Tales from the Elvenpath (2004)

Drakkar took the opportunity to release *Tales from the Elvenpath* in 2004 to capitalise on the band's enormous *Once* era. The song selection was mostly sound, taking in signature tracks such as 'Sleeping Sun', 'Sacrament of Wilderness' and 'Over the Hills and Far Away' as well as a tempting batch of rarities including 'Nightquest', 'Sleepwalker' and *Century Child* B-sides 'Lagoon' and 'The Wayfarer'. Despite its title, however, 'Elvenpath' is not included due to Drakkar only retaining rights for post-*Oceanborn* releases.

In the band's *Once Upon a Nightwish* biography, Tuomas pulled no punches when discussing the release:

> The song selection is just fine, but the cover art is horrible, and the whole idea of putting out a 'greatest hits' compilation at the time was just stupid. On the other hand, you always have to look at things from many angles – if I was Boggi, I would've probably done the same thing. Just think about it: you've worked hard to make the band successful in Europe, put lots of work and money into the group, and suddenly the band leaves the label and Nuclear Blast gets to reap the profits.

Regardless of the band's thoughts, the album charted in Austria, Germany, and Switzerland. *Once* had steered the group's sound to a more cinematic future and, in retrospect, it was a fitting time to look back on the band's earlier years. Nuclear Blast agreed, following up *Once*'s success with their own, more comprehensive compilation.

Bestwishes (2005)

Just as Drakkar had done for Germany and Europe, Japanese label Toy's Factory also made the most of Nightwish's expanding mid-noughties success. Unlike its European predecessor, *Bestwishes* was also able to incorporate songs from the band's debut, lifting the defiant 'Beauty and the Beast' but also the comparative curveball 'Know Why the Nightingale Sings'. Appealing to Japan's penchant for power metal, the spirited 'The Riddler' and 'Crownless' were notable choices amongst the majority of singles and other fan favourites. The compilation reached the top 250 in Japan, shifting over a thousand copies in its first week, though not a patch on the near 10,000 sales of *Once* the year prior.

Highest Hopes: The Best of Nightwish (2005)
A symbol of the band's success, *Highest Hopes: The Best of Nightwish* became the third Nightwish compilation released in two years though it stood out as easily the most essential. Curated and released with the band's label Nuclear Blast, it came with an unspoken endorsement from the band and a modest selection of exclusives – a 2005 re-record of 'Sleeping Sun' and a live cover recording of Pink Floyd's 'High Hopes'. The tracklist was a fair assemblage of essential singles ('Nemo', 'Ever Dream'), solid album cuts ('Stargazers', 'Dead Boy's Poem') and the aforementioned new recordings, propelling it to number one in the Finnish and Mexican album charts. Interestingly, it almost surpassed the chart peak of *Bestwishes* in Japan, scraping in at 235 on the Japanese album charts, bolstered by a second disc of rarities and live tracks as well as an extended DVD featuring performances from 2002's Summer Breeze festival.

The Sound of Nightwish Reborn (2008)
Dark Passion Play saw Nightwish lock their focus on America like never before. As well as a lengthy number of US dates during the album's supporting tour, a digital-only compilation was released by the band's US label, Roadrunner Records. Though the EP didn't offer any new tracks, it was a virtual gathering of the B-sides from the album's singles, including the demo versions of 'The Poet and the Pendulum', 'Eva' and 'Amaranth' and the phenomenally well received originals 'Escapist' and 'While Your Lips Are Still Red'.

Walking In the Air: The Ballads (2011)
Walking in The Air: The Ballads followed seven years after Drakkar's previous compilation *Tales from the Elvenpath*. The collection suffered twofold as the German label homed in on the band's expanding audience but were only able to include material from *Century Child* and earlier – already, it rendered the content somewhat dated, but it was the concept of gathering all the band's slowest tracks that felt like the biggest crime. The release lacked dynamism and whilst many of the striking ballads were able to shine on the group's prior studio releases, the collection stripped much of their charm by combining them into an exhausting slog.

Imaginaerum: The Score (2012)
Compilation is a loose descriptor of the score for *Imaginaerum*, the band's movie in collaboration with director Stobe Harju. Many of the compositions will sound familiar, having been lifted from the Nightwish album released a year before, this time reworked to meet the needs of the film. Almost all the

vocals have been stripped out, save for 'Deeper Down' which reinterprets 'The Crow, The Owl and The Dove'.

Petri Alanko produced *Imaginaerum: The Score* alongside Tuomas and was tasked with turning the cinematic metal into a cinema-ready soundtrack – clearly, the Finn impressed as the band invited him back to reimagine the first two singles from *Endless Forms Most Beautiful*. As was a familiar trend, the score managed its highest chart position in the band's home country, where it peaked just outside the top ten.

Decades (2018)

Twenty years in the making, *Decades* truly is the most comprehensive, essential compilation in the band's catalogue. For the first time, it was Tuomas himself that was involved in the song selection, emphasising many times that the collection is not a 'best-of', but rather a gathering of the most quintessential songs from across the band's history.

With Floor Jansen solidifying her place as the band's frontwoman, many expected that the album would include re-recordings of past Nightwish material, something the group quickly confirmed would not be the case. The songs were remastered for the release, ensuring Tarja, Anette, Sami and Jukka were rightly still present in the celebratory retrospective. Compiled in reverse-timeline order – bravely chucking out 'The Greatest Show on Earth' as the daunting opening cut – the most unexpected addition was the final track, a recording of 'Nightwish' from the band's very first demo.

Cementing *Decades* as the ultimate Nightwish collection, it was supported by a world tour that sought to return some old favourites into the setlist, incorporating tracks from every Nightwish album to date as the band traversed the globe once more across over eighty shows.

Live Releases

From Wishes to Eternity (2001)

If any live release was drained to a husk for content, it was *From Wishes to Eternity*, recorded in Tampere. Released in both DVD and VHS formats, the audio recordings were issued on CD as well as reinforcing the tracklist of multiple editions of the *Over the Hills and Far Away* EP, which dropped months later.

The set covered the band's power metal peak on the *Wishmaster* tour, inviting along Sonata Arctica's Tony Kakko for 'Beauty and the Beast' and regular collaborator Tapio Wilska on 'The Pharaoh Sails to Orion'. Highlights include the one-two punch of 'The Kinslayer' and 'She Is My Sin', the final part of the lengthy 'FantasMic' and a short medley of Tuomas' cinematic muses: Hans Zimmer's score for 1995's *Crimson Deep* and Trevor Rabin's contributions to 1999 horror *Deep Blue Sea.*

The biggest surprise was an omission, the comparatively underrated 'Swanheart' scoring the lucrative ballad spot instead of favourite 'Sleeping Sun'. The single was instead included as a bonus music video alongside 'The Carpenter', the disappointing 'Sacrament of Wilderness' clip wisely absent from the band's videography to date.

End of Innocence (2003)

Documentaries have long become a standard for Nightwish live releases – from the introduction of Floor Jansen on *Showtime, Storytime's* 'Please Learn the Setlist in 48 Hours', to the wistful hindsight of Tarja's impending departure on *A Day Before Tomorrow. End of Innocence* is an outlier in that it presented the documentary not as bonus content but as the main draw, throwing in a few live tracks to sweeten the deal.

If Nightwish onstage had hidden behind the haughtiness of an operatic frontwoman, *End of Innocence* took great pleasure in uncovering the chaotic humanity that was lingering behind the scenes; the very man who penned the group's poetic gems seen carried into an elevator in a drunken stupor and the newly inducted bassist later stripping to his underwear and dressing as a prank-spurned angel. *Century Child* was a notoriously difficult period for Tuomas in particular, echoes of the tension permeating the interviews and recordings that comprise the two-hour feature, but thankfully the film manages an earnest reflection of the ups and downs of being in a successful metal band and steers away from lingering too long in the gloom.

Live footage completed the package, a couple of particular gems standing out in the tracklists: from a 2003 performance in Norway, the band's cover of 'Wild Child' was one of five inclusions, whilst the Summer Breeze performance filmed in 2002 gave an audience to the oft-overlooked treasure '10th Man Down'. Ever the ones to circumvent usual marketing strategies, their final stab at luring in buyers came with the DVD's promise of an 'extremely confusing photo gallery' which offered a risky click between a striking live shot or a naked bandmember in the sauna – the end of innocence, indeed.

End of an Era (2006)
The show that shook Nightwish fans to their core, Nightwish's triumphant performance in Helsinki proved to be their last with Tarja, handing her the infamous open letter and announcing her dismissal immediately after the show. Upon *End of an Era*'s release, it was approached with a voyeuristic curiosity – every shot of the band being analysed to spot clues for the aftermath to follow – but time solidified the release as a genuinely remarkable performance, regardless of the drama that surrounded it. It was no huge surprise when the live release received an official reissue from Nuclear Blast twelve years later.

Sandwiched between a Hans Zimmer intro and outro, the band's cinematic sound found a home on the massive Hartwall Arena stage. Be it the soothing 'Kuolema Tekee Taiteilijan' or the bombast of 'Planet Hell', the band's prior material is revitalised by their widening scope, anthems such as 'Wishmaster' and 'The Kinslayer' sounding more explosive than ever before. The set builds to a two-part finale: the meditative resonance of 'Creek Mary's Blood' with guest John Two-Hawks and the feelgood climax of 'Over the Hills and Far Away' and 'Wish I Had an Angel'.

Just as Jansen's 'Ghost Love Score' performance propelled Nightwish into the attentions of YouTube reactors, 'The Phantom of the Opera' was another favourite for the online community to offer their thoughts and inevitable gushing. As of 2022, it's the latter that has racked up the most views on YouTube, surpassing thirty-one million in just two years.

Made in Hong Kong (and in Various Other Places) (2009)
The band's most momentous live release was eventually followed by their most underwhelming. Following the introduction of Anette Olzon, fans were clamouring to hear her takes on the Tarja era tracks that had peppered the sets of the *Dark Passion Play* world tour. The cobbled-together tracklist felt unsure of its own intent – seven live tracks from various tour dates, a smattering of demos (including an unreleased early stab at 'Cadence of her Last Breath') and the album's two original B-sides 'Escapist' and 'While Your Lips Are Still Red'. The DVD didn't fare much better, the standard inclusion of the promo videos for the album's singles and a short documentary that, whilst giving an insight into Anette's settling into the band, didn't offer much of note. Disappointingly, due to her exit before the recording of *Showtime, Storytime*, no live release with Anette was ever officially released, souring *Made in Hong Kong (and in Various Other Places)* even further with a persistent pondering of what could have been.

Showtime, Storytime (2013)

By 2012, it was expected that an expansive tour would soon be followed by a DVD release, as had been the case since as far back as the *Wishmaster* days. It was an effective and lucrative way to tide over the swathes of fans in the ever-growing periods between Nightwish studio records, but neither fans nor the band foresaw the explosion of *Showtime, Storytime* into one of the defining moments in the band's career.

A headline set from the renowned Wacken festival, the DVD had all the makings of a Nightwish spectacle – an ocean of enraptured fans, an enormous stage crowned with the festival's signature bullhead and plenty of space to blast pyro and show off their euphoric light show. The setlist was also ideal, though technically the band were touring the *Imaginaerum* album, it was a satisfying mix of the band's career to date. Flying through highlights of previous tours ('Ever Dream', 'Dark Chest of Wonders') and the best live cuts from the recent record ('Last Ride of the Day', 'Storytime'), the performance felt like a band at the peak of their success, a greatest hits set comprised of modern metal classics, all underscored by the exhilarated crowd.

It's clear to see why people wanted in on the Nightwish phenomenon, and what better way than to experience the band's truest masterpiece, 'Ghost Love Score'. Much has been said already about the performance given by Floor Jansen, transforming the song into a magnificent showcase of her vocal versatility, the epic building tirelessly to the spine-tingling moment in which the crowd erupt to celebrate the song's stunning crescendo. It is arguably *the* quintessential Nightwish moment, capturing the passion of both a band that had once again battled against the odds and their loyal audience, utterly enthralled by every second.

Vehicle of Spirit (2016)

Vehicle of Spirit takes its title from a metaphor used by Troy Donockley's friend to describe the Nightwish live show. From the small-scale pyro on *From Wishes to Eternity*, the visual presentation of a Nightwish show had evolved drastically – as the venues grew bigger, so did the pyros, the curated video backdrops and the personnel required to pull it all off. The DVD celebrates two landmark performances for the group: their biggest spectacle to date in Tampere, quite literally bursting with pyro and fireworks, and the acclaimed Wembley show, which crowned them as the first Finnish group to sell out the arena in its history. The venue held a significance for Tuomas, as he told Ticketmaster ahead of the date:

> When our manager told us for the first time about a month ago, I had a huge incredulous smile on my face. It took a while for us to absorb what was going to happen. Even the word 'Wembley' has a mystical aura around it, and once we reach the 19th of December, it´ll be one of those wonderful, once-in-a-lifetime moments.

One thing Tuomas and the band kept to themselves was a special guest appearance from Richard Dawkins. The response from the audience that greeted the biologist may have even eclipsed the roars reserved for the band, the guest spot rounding out yet another bucket-list ticking Nightwish performance.

If one small criticism could be cast towards the momentous shows, it's their relatively similar setlists. Both lifted from the same tour, it would admittedly prove a near-impossible decision to immortalise only one and have to sacrifice Wembley's long-awaited Jansen take of 'The Poet and the Pendulum' or Tampere's stirring renditions of 'The Islander' and 'Sleeping Sun'. The offering is plentiful, particularly for fans of 'Élan', 'Yours Is an Empty Hope' and 'Weak Fantasy', which boasted three inclusions across the bundle's triple DVD set.

Nuclear Blast were certainly in a generous mood during the curation of *Vehicle of Spirit*, with ten additional performances thrown in on a third disc, including the acoustic live debut of 'Edema Ruh' and the Tony Kakko duet 'Last Ride of the Day' from Brazil's Rock in Rio festival. All this wrapped in a package that was something of a departure for the group's usual artistic choices, complete with a subtle tease for their upcoming anniversary celebrations as it proudly remarked '20 years in the making' on the theatrical cover.

Decades: Live in Buenos Aires (2019)

Said celebrations were marked by the Decades world tour, delving deep into the Nightwish archives to celebrate their twenty years of existence. Coinciding with the release of the compilation of the same name, the setlist for the tour primarily included songs from *Decades*, though padded out with a hefty dose of *Wishmaster* tracks ('Come Cover Me', 'Deep Silent Complete' and, on some dates, 'Wishmaster' itself) and the unexpected intro of *Oceanborn*'s 'Swanheart'.

The tour dates were altered slightly for the European leg of the tour, kicking off with the winning 'Dark Chest of Wonders' and incorporating live favourite 'Last Ride of the Day'. *Decades: Live in Buenos Aires* is taken from the third leg of the tour, just shy of these changes, but wisely chosen for the thunderous reception afforded by Latin American fans. It's this audience that elevates the live release, much lighter on pyro and visual effects than the band's previous output – instead, the recording is bursting with an energy and enthusiasm of loyal Nightwish fans, a felicitous sight for the celebratory victory lap of the *Decades* world tour.

Also available from Sonicbond

Opeth - *on track*

every album, every song

Jordan Blum
Paperback
144 pages
40 colour photographs
978-1-78951-166-5
£15.99
$22.95

Every album and every song by these Swedish metal legends.

There has never been – and never will be – another band like Opeth. Formed in Stockholm, Sweden around 1989, their thirty-year career showcases a melding of diverse influences. They demonstrate a commitment to both songwriting and instrumental excellence, not to mention stylistic diversity – no matter what the cost – that's unmatched by any of their stylistic peers. Whether it be their unashamedly brutal early LPs, their near-faultless mid-period opuses, or their somewhat polarising recent glimpses into macabre 1970s-esque prog/jazz rock eccentricity, mastermind Mikael Åkerfeldt and company continuously create records that push themselves, their audience, and progressive music as a whole, forward. The result is among the most extraordinary, dependable, and laudable legacies in modern metal.

Using a meticulously crafted mixture of original analysis and behind-the-scenes research, this book digs into all facets of Opeth's output to discover how they innovated and evolved with practically every release. After all, each 'observation' – from their 1990s black metal classics (*Morningrise* and *My Arms, Your Hearse*) and 2000s progressive death metal masterpieces (*Blackwater Park* and *Ghost Reveries*) to their stunning progressive rock/jazz fusion excursions of the 2010s (*Pale Communion* and *In Cauda Venenum*) – found Opeth ceaselessly harvesting a one-of-a-kind catalogue that remains remarkably influential and impressive.

Also available from Sonicbond

On Track series

Alan Parsons Project – Steve Swift 978-1-78952-154-2
Tori Amos – Lisa Torem 978-1-78952-142-9
Asia – Peter Braidis 978-1-78952-099-6
Badfinger – Robert Day-Webb 978-1-878952-176-4
Barclay James Harvest – Keith and Monica Domone 978-1-78952-067-5
The Beatles – Andrew Wild 978-1-78952-009-5
The Beatles Solo 1969-1980 – Andrew Wild 978-1-78952-030-9
Blue Oyster Cult – Jacob Holm-Lupo 978-1-78952-007-1
Blur – Matt Bishop – 978-178952-164-1
Marc Bolan and T.Rex – Peter Gallagher 978-1-78952-124-5
Kate Bush – Bill Thomas 978-1-78952-097-2
Camel – Hamish Kuzminski 978-1-78952-040-8
Caravan – Andy Boot 978-1-78952-127-6
Cardiacs – Eric Benac 978-1-78952-131-3
Eric Clapton Solo – Andrew Wild 978-1-78952-141-2
The Clash – Nick Assirati 978-1-78952-077-4
Crosby, Stills and Nash – Andrew Wild 978-1-78952-039-2
The Damned – Morgan Brown 978-1-78952-136-8
Deep Purple and Rainbow 1968-79 – Steve Pilkington 978-1-78952-002-6
Dire Straits – Andrew Wild 978-1-78952-044-6
The Doors – Tony Thompson 978-1-78952-137-5
Dream Theater – Jordan Blum 978-1-78952-050-7
Electric Light Orchestra – Barry Delve 978-1-78952-152-8
Elvis Costello and The Attractions – Georg Purvis 978-1-78952-129-0
Emerson Lake and Palmer – Mike Goode 978-1-78952-000-2
Fairport Convention – Kevan Furbank 978-1-78952-051-4
Peter Gabriel – Graeme Scarfe 978-1-78952-138-2
Genesis – Stuart MacFarlane 978-1-78952-005-7
Gentle Giant – Gary Steel 978-1-78952-058-3
Gong – Kevan Furbank 978-1-78952-082-8
Hall and Oates – Ian Abrahams 978-1-78952-167-2
Hawkwind – Duncan Harris 978-1-78952-052-1
Peter Hammill – Richard Rees Jones 978-1-78952-163-4
Roy Harper – Opher Goodwin 978-1-78952-130-6
Jimi Hendrix – Emma Stott 978-1-78952-175-7
The Hollies – Andrew Darlington 978-1-78952-159-7
Iron Maiden – Steve Pilkington 978-1-78952-061-3
Jefferson Airplane – Richard Butterworth 978-1-78952-143-6
Jethro Tull – Jordan Blum 978-1-78952-016-3
Elton John in the 1970s – Peter Kearns 978-1-78952-034-7
The Incredible String Band – Tim Moon 978-1-78952-107-8
Iron Maiden – Steve Pilkington 978-1-78952-061-3
Judas Priest – John Tucker 978-1-78952-018-7
Kansas – Kevin Cummings 978-1-78952-057-6
The Kinks – Martin Hutchinson 978-1-78952-172-6
Korn – Matt Karpe 978-1-78952-153-5
Led Zeppelin – Steve Pilkington 978-1-78952-151-1
Level 42 – Matt Philips 978-1-78952-102-3

Little Feat – 978-1-78952-168-9
Aimee Mann – Jez Rowden 978-1-78952-036-1
Joni Mitchell – Peter Kearns 978-1-78952-081-1
The Moody Blues – Geoffrey Feakes 978-1-78952-042-2
Motorhead – Duncan Harris 978-1-78952-173-3
Mike Oldfield – Ryan Yard 978-1-78952-060-6
Opeth – Jordan Blum 978-1-78-952-166-5
Tom Petty – Richard James 978-1-78952-128-3
Porcupine Tree – Nick Holmes 978-1-78952-144-3
Queen – Andrew Wild 978-1-78952-003-3
Radiohead – William Allen 978-1-78952-149-8
Renaissance – David Detmer 978-1-78952-062-0
The Rolling Stones 1963-80 – Steve Pilkington 978-1-78952-017-0
The Smiths and Morrissey – Tommy Gunnarsson 978-1-78952-140-5
Status Quo the Frantic Four Years – Richard James 978-1-78952-160-3
Steely Dan – Jez Rowden 978-1-78952-043-9
Steve Hackett – Geoffrey Feakes 978-1-78952-098-9
Thin Lizzy – Graeme Stroud 978-1-78952-064-4
Toto – Jacob Holm-Lupo 978-1-78952-019-4
U2 – Eoghan Lyng 978-1-78952-078-1
UFO – Richard James 978-1-78952-073-6
The Who – Geoffrey Feakes 978-1-78952-076-7
Roy Wood and the Move – James R Turner 978-1-78952-008-8
Van Der Graaf Generator – Dan Coffey 978-1-78952-031-6
Yes – Stephen Lambe 978-1-78952-001-9
Frank Zappa 1966 to 1979 – Eric Benac 978-1-78952-033-0
Warren Zevon – Peter Gallagher 978-1-78952-170-2
10CC – Peter Kearns 978-1-78952-054-5

Decades Series

The Bee Gees in the 1960s – Andrew Môn Hughes et al 978-1-78952-148-1
The Bee Gees in the 1970s – Andrew Môn Hughes et al 978-1-78952-179-5
Black Sabbath in the 1970s – Chris Sutton 978-1-78952-171-9
Britpop – Peter Richard Adams and Matt Pooler 978-1-78952-169-6
Alice Cooper in the 1970s – Chris Sutton 978-1-78952-104-7
Curved Air in the 1970s – Laura Shenton 978-1-78952-069-9
Bob Dylan in the 1980s – Don Klees 978-1-78952-157-3
Fleetwood Mac in the 1970s – Andrew Wild 978-1-78952-105-4
Focus in the 1970s – Stephen Lambe 978-1-78952-079-8
Free and Bad Company in the 1970s – John Van der Kiste 978-1-78952-178-8
Genesis in the 1970s – Bill Thomas 978178952-146-7
George Harrison in the 1970s – Eoghan Lyng 978-1-78952-174-0
Marillion in the 1980s – Nathaniel Webb 978-1-78952-065-1
Mott the Hoople and Ian Hunter in the 1970s – John Van der Kiste 978-1-78-952-162-7
Pink Floyd In The 1970s – Georg Purvis 978-1-78952-072-9
Tangerine Dream in the 1970s – Stephen Palmer 978-1-78952-161-0
The Sweet in the 1970s – Darren Johnson from Gary Cosby collection 978-1-78952-139-9

Uriah Heep in the 1970s – Steve Pilkington 978-1-78952-103-0
Yes in the 1980s – Stephen Lambe with David Watkinson 978-1-78952-125-2

On Screen series

Carry On… – Stephen Lambe 978-1-78952-004-0
David Cronenberg – Patrick Chapman 978-1-78952-071-2
Doctor Who: The David Tennant Years – Jamie Hailstone 978-1-78952-066-8
James Bond – Andrew Wild – 978-1-78952-010-1
Monty Python – Steve Pilkington 978-1-78952-047-7
Seinfeld Seasons 1 to 5 – Stephen Lambe 978-1-78952-012-5

Other Books

1967: A Year In Psychedelic Rock – Kevan Furbank 978-1-78952-155-9
1970: A Year In Rock – John Van der Kiste 978-1-78952-147-4
1973: The Golden Year of Progressive Rock 978-1-78952-165-8
Babysitting A Band On The Rocks – G.D. Praetorius 978-1-78952-106-1
Eric Clapton Sessions – Andrew Wild 978-1-78952-177-1
Derek Taylor: For Your Radioactive Children – Andrew Darlington 978-1-78952-038-5
The Golden Road: The Recording History of The Grateful Dead – John Kilbride 978-1-78952-156-6
Iggy and The Stooges On Stage 1967-1974 – Per Nilsen 978-1-78952-101-6
Jon Anderson and the Warriors – the road to Yes – David Watkinson 978-1-78952-059-0
Nu Metal: A Definitive Guide – Matt Karpe 978-1-78952-063-7
Tommy Bolin: In and Out of Deep Purple – Laura Shenton 978-1-78952-070-5
Maximum Darkness – Deke Leonard 978-1-78952-048-4
Maybe I Should've Stayed In Bed – Deke Leonard 978-1-78952-053-8
The Twang Dynasty – Deke Leonard 978-1-78952-049-1

and many more to come!

Would you like to write for Sonicbond Publishing?

At Sonicbond Publishing we are always on the look-out for authors, particularly for our two main series:

On Track. Mixing fact with in depth analysis, the On Track series examines the work of a particular musical artist or group. All genres are considered from easy listening and jazz to 60s soul to 90s pop, via rock and metal.

On Screen. This series looks at the world of film and television. Subjects considered include directors, actors and writers, as well as entire television and film series. As with the On Track series, we balance fact with analysis.

While professional writing experience would, of course, be an advantage the most important qualification is to have real enthusiasm and knowledge of your subject. First-time authors are welcomed, but the ability to write well in English is essential.

Sonicbond Publishing has distribution throughout Europe and North America, and all books are also published in E-book form. Authors will be paid a royalty based on sales of their book.

Further details are available from www.sonicbondpublishing.co.uk. To contact us, complete the contact form there or email info@sonicbondpublishing.co.uk